CliffsNotes™

Ellison's
Invisible Man

By Durthy A. Washington

IN THIS BOOK

- ■ Learn about the Life and Background of the Author
- ■ Preview an Introduction to the Novel
- ■ Explore themes, literary devices, and character insight in the Critical Commentaries
- ■ Examine in-depth Character Analyses
- ■ Understand the nuances of the novel with Critical Essays
- ■ Reinforce what you learn with CliffsNotes Review
- ■ Find additional information to further your study in CliffsNotes Resource Center and online at www.cliffsnotes.com

D0370308

IDG Books Worldwide, Inc.
An International Data Group Company
Foster City, CA • Chicago, IL • Indianapolis, IN • New York, NY

About the Author

Durthy A. Washington is a writer whose area of special interest is American ethnic literature, with an emphasis on the works of black American authors. She holds a master's degree in education from the University of Southern California and a master's degree in English from San Jose State University. She currently teaches at the U.S. Air Force Academy in Colorado Springs, Colorado.

Publisher's Acknowledgments

Editorial

Project Editor: Gregg Summers
Acquisitions Editor: Greg Tubach
Copy Editor: Esmeralda St. Clair
Glossary Editors: The editors and staff at Webster's New World™ Dictionaries
Editorial Administrator: Michelle Hacker
Editorial Assistant: Jennifer Young

Production

Proofreader and Indexer: York Production Services
IDG Books Indianapolis Production Department

CliffsNotes™ Ellison's *Invisible Man*
Published by
IDG Books Worldwide, Inc.
An International Data Group Company
919 E. Hillsdale Blvd.
Suite 300
Foster City, CA 94404
www.idgbooks.com (IDG Books Worldwide Web site)
www.cliffsnotes.com (CliffsNotes Web site)

Library of Congress Control Number: 00-107795

ISBN: 0-7645-8656-4

Printed in the United States of America

10 9 8 7 6 5 4 3 2 1

1O/QV/RS/QQ/IN

Distributed in the United States by IDG Books Worldwide, Inc.

Distributed by CDG Books Canada Inc. for Canada; by Transworld Publishers Limited in the United Kingdom; by IDG Norge Books for Norway; by IDG Sweden Books for Sweden; by IDG Books Australia Publishing Corporation Pty. Ltd. for Australia and New Zealand; by TransQuest Publishers Pte Ltd. for Singapore, Malaysia, Thailand, Indonesia, and Hong Kong; by Gotop Information Inc. for Taiwan; by ICG Muse, Inc. for Japan; by Norma Comunicaciones S.A. for Columbia; by Intersoft for South Africa; by Eyrolles for France; by International Thomson Publishing for Germany, Austria and Switzerland; by Distribuidora Cuspide for Argentina; by LR International for Brazil; by Galileo Libros for Chile; by Ediciones ZETA S.C.R. Ltda. for Peru; by WS Computer Publishing Corporation, Inc., for the Philippines; by Contemporanea de Ediciones for Venezuela; by Express Computer Distributors for the Caribbean and West Indies; by Micronesia Media Distributor, Inc. for Micronesia; by Grupo Editorial Norma S.A. for Guatemala; by Chips Computadoras S.A. de C.V. for Mexico; by Editorial Norma de Panama S.A. for Panama; by American Bookshops for Finland. Authorized Sales Agent: Anthony Rudkin Associates for the Middle East and North Africa.

For general information on IDG Books Worldwide's books in the U.S., please call our Consumer Customer Service department at **800-762-2974**. For reseller information, including discounts and premium sales, please call our Reseller Customer Service department at **800-434-3422**.

For information on where to purchase IDG Books Worldwide's books outside the U.S., please contact our International Sales department at **317-572-3993** or fax **317-572-4002**.

For consumer information on foreign language translations, please contact our Customer Service department at **1-800-434-3422**, fax **317-572-4002**, or e-mail rights@idgbooks.com.

For information on licensing foreign or domestic rights, please phone **+1-650-653-7098**.

For sales inquiries and special prices for bulk quantities, please contact our Order Services department at **800-434-3422** or write to the address above.

For information on using IDG Books Worldwide's books in the classroom or for ordering examination copies, please contact our Educational Sales department at **800-434-2086** or fax **317-572-4005**.

For press review copies, author interviews, or other publicity information, please contact our Public Relations department at **650-653-7000** or fax **650-653-7500**.

For authorization to photocopy items for corporate, personal, or educational use, please contact Copyright Clearance Center, 222 Rosewood Drive, Danvers, MA 01923, or fax **978-750-4470**.

Table of Contents

Life and Background of the Author 1
Personal Background 2
Career Highlights 3
Literary Influences 4
Commenting on Blacks in America 5

Introduction to the Novel 7
Introduction 8
A Brief Synopsis 11
List of Characters 13
Character Map 19

Critical Commentaries 21
Prologue 22
  Summary 22
  Commentary 23
  Glossary 24
Chapter 1 26
  Summary 26
  Commentary 26
  Glossary 29
Chapter 2 30
  Summary 30
  Commentary 30
  Glossary 32
Chapters 3–4 34
  Summary 34
  Commentary 35
  Glossary 37
Chapters 5–6 39
  Summary 39
  Commentary 39
  Glossary 41
Chapters 7–9 43
  Summary 43
  Commentary 44
  Glossary 46
Chapters 10–12 48
  Summary 48
  Commentary 49
  Glossary 51

Chapter 13 52
    Summary 52
    Commentary 53
    Glossary 54
Chapters 14–16 55
    Summary 55
    Commentary 57
    Glossary 58
Chapter 17 60
    Summary 60
    Commentary 60
    Glossary 63
Chapters 18–19 64
    Summary 64
    Commentary 65
    Glossary 66
Chapters 20–21 67
    Summary 67
    Commentary 67
    Glossary 70
Chapter 22 71
    Summary 71
    Commentary 71
    Glossary 73
Chapter 23 74
    Summary 74
    Commentary 75
    Glossary 76
Chapter 24 77
    Summary 77
    Commentary 77
    Glossary 79
Chapter 25 80
    Summary 80
    Commentary 81
    Glossary 83
Epilogue 84
    Summary 84
    Commentary 84
    Glossary 85

Character Analyses **87**

   The Narrator 88

   Mr. Norton 89

   Dr. A. Hebert Bledsoe 90

   Rev. Homer A. Barbee 91

   Jim Trueblood 92

   Ras the Exhorter 93

   Mary Rambo 94

   Brother Tod Clifton 95

   Brother Jack 96

Critical Essays **97**

   Symbols and Symbolism in *Invisible Man* 98

   Wordplay in *Invisible Man* 102

   Profiles of Leadership in *Invisible Man* 104

   Harlem: City of Dreams 107

Cliffs Notes Review **109**

   Q&A 109

   Identify the Quote 110

   Essay Questions 111

   Practice Projects 111

Cliffs Notes Resource Center **113**

   Books 113

   Internet 114

   Journal Resource 115

   Send Us Your Favorite Tips 115

Index **117**

How to Use This Book

CliffsNotes *Invisible Man* supplements the original work, giving you background information about the author, an introduction to the novel, a graphical character map, critical commentaries, expanded glossaries, and a comprehensive index. CliffsNotes Review tests your comprehension of the original text and reinforces learning with questions and answers, practice projects, and more. For further information on Ralph Ellison and *Invisible Man*, check out the CliffsNotes Resource Center.

CliffsNotes provides the following icons to highlight essential elements of particular interest:

Reveals the underlying themes in the work.

Helps you to more easily relate to or discover the depth of a character.

Uncovers elements such as setting, atmosphere, mystery, passion, violence, irony, symbolism, tragedy, foreshadowing, and satire.

Enables you to appreciate the nuances of words and phrases.

Don't Miss Our Web Site

Discover classic literature as well as modern-day treasures by visiting the CliffsNotes Web site at www.cliffsnotes.com. You can obtain a quick download of a CliffsNotes title, purchase a title in print form, browse our catalog, or view online samples.

You'll also find interactive tools that are fun and informative, links to interesting Web sites, tips, articles, and additional resources to help you, not only for literature, but for test prep, finance, careers, computers, and Internet too. See you at www.cliffsnotes.com!

LIFE AND BACKGROUND OF THE AUTHOR

Personal Background 2

Career Highlights .3

Literary Influences 4

Commenting on Blacks in America 5

Personal Background

Ralph Waldo Ellison was born March 1, 1914, in Oklahoma City, Oklahoma, to Lewis Alfred Ellison, a construction foreman who died when Ellison was only three years old, and the former Ida Milsap, a church stewardess, who used to bring him books she borrowed from the houses she cleaned. Ellison attended Frederick Douglass School in Oklahoma City, receiving lessons in symphonic composition. He began playing the trumpet at age eight and, at age eighteen, attended Tuskegee Institute in Montgomery, Alabama, studying music from 1933 to 1936. During that time, he worked at a variety of jobs including janitor, shoeshine boy, jazz musician, and freelance photographer. He also became a game hunter to keep himself alive, a skill he says he learned from reading Hemingway.

Completing only three years majoring in music at Tuskegee, Ellison sometimes referred to himself as a college dropout. Ironically, Ellison went on to receive 12 honorary doctorate degrees from such prestigious universities as Tuskegee Institute, Rutgers University, the University of Michigan, and Harvard University.

Moving to New York in 1936, Ellison met writers Richard Wright and Langston Hughes, which led to his first attempts at fiction and prompted his move to Harlem where he lived for more than 40 years with his wife, Fanny McConnell.

A renowned novelist, short story writer, and critic, Ellison taught at several colleges and universities and lectured extensively at such prestigious institutions as Yale University, the Library of Congress, and the U.S. Military Academy.

In 1970, Ellison became Albert Schweitzer Professor of the Humanities at New York University, where he served until 1980. He also received the prestigious Chevalier de L'Ordre des Artes et Lettres, one of the highest honors France can bestow on a foreign writer. In 1982, he was named professor emeritus at NYU, teaching for several years while continuing to write.

Ellison died of cancer on April 16, 1994, at his home in New York City.

Career Highlights

Soon after his move to New York in 1936, his book reviews, short stories, and articles began to appear in numerous magazines and anthologies, and Ellison was on his way to becoming an acclaimed author.

Early Success with *Invisible Man*

In the early 1940s, Ellison started out writing a novel about a captured American pilot in a Nazi prisoner-of-war camp. But during the summer of 1945, visiting friends in Vermont while on sick leave from the Merchant Marine, the opening lines of *Invisible Man* came to him, prompting him to write an entirely different novel.

Ellison described *Invisible Man*, published in 1952, as "a novel about innocence and human error, a struggle through illusion to reality." Ellison claimed that his novel comprised "a series of reversals," providing a "portrait of the artist as rabble-rouser." Responding to questions concerning the narrator's journey as a reflection of the black struggle for justice and equality, Ellison contended that he is "not concerned with injustice, but with art," pointing out that there is "no dichotomy between art and protest." To illustrate, he cited works such as Cervantes' *Don Quixote* and Dostoyevski's *Notes from Underground*, arguing that these literary works not only embody protest against social and political constraints, but ultimately protest against the limitations of human life itself.

Ellison became known primarily for *Invisible Man*, which won the Russwurm Award and the National Book Award and established him as one of the most important American authors of the twentieth century. But he also published several nonfiction works and short stories.

Other Major Works

In 1960, Ellison published his first Hickman stories, "And Hickman Arrives" and "The Roof, the Steeple, and the People." In these stories, he introduced Senator Adam "Bliss" Sunraider, a light-skinned black man, passing for white most of his adult life, and Reverend "Daddy" Hickman, the Negro preacher who takes him in and raises him as his own son.

Ellison also published two important volumes of nonfiction, *Shadow and Act* (1964) and *Going to the Territory* (1986). These two works, together with numerous unpublished speeches and writings, were published in 1995 as *The Collected Essays of Ralph Ellison*. He also wrote numerous short stories—including "King of the Bingo Game," "That I Had the Wings," and "Flying Home"—published posthumously in 1996 as *Flying Home and Other Stories*.

The Hickman characters later appeared in his posthumously published novel, *Juneteenth*. Because 368 pages of his Hickman manuscript were destroyed in a fire at his summer home in Massachusetts in 1967, Ellison spent the remaining years of his life reconstructing it. The novel, still incomplete at his death, was eventually published as *Juneteenth*.

Literary Influences

Ellison credits T.S. Eliot's poem, *The Waste Land*—which he describes "as intriguing as a trumpet improvisation by Louis Armstrong," for arousing his interest in literature. Trying to gain a better understanding, Ellison started reading literary criticism. He soon started searching for what he called "Eliot's kind of sensibility" in Negro poetry but didn't find it—until he came across the writings of Richard Wright.

Although he admired Wright's work, such as the novel *Native Son*, Ellison felt that Wright's use of the *protest novel*, which generally depicted blacks as the oppressed victims of whites, and his tendency to write primarily for a white audience limited his vision. Writing *Invisible Man*, Ellison set out to move beyond the protest novel to portray a narrator whose life was not defined strictly by his race, but by his willingness to accept personal responsibility for creating his own life.

Adopting His Namesake's Philosophy

Like his namesake, poet and essayist Ralph Waldo Emerson (1803–82), Ellison believed in the philosophy of transcendentalism, asserting that individuals create their own reality and that reality is essentially mental or spiritual in nature. This accounts for much of his fascination with masks and disguises and his preoccupation with appearance vs. reality.

Ellison admired the American transcendentalists, particularly Emerson, Whitman, and Thoreau. He liked their faith in the American democratic ideal, concern for cultural pluralism, belief in personal freedom, and idealistic vision of a world in which individuals would transcend (or rise above) their petty desires for self-aggrandizement, obtain a kind of spiritual enlightenment, and work together for the good of all people. This goal is perhaps best expressed in Emerson's essay, "Self-Reliance," contending that, "Nothing is at last sacred but the integrity of your own mind," emphasizing the virtues of solitude by declaring that "the great man is he who in the midst of the crowd keeps with perfect sweetness the independence of solitude."

From Poetry to Novels

In a 1954 interview, Ellison contended that by devoting himself to the novel, he "took on one of the responsibilities inherited by those who practice the craft in the U.S.: that of describing for all that fragment of the huge diverse American experience which I know best, and which offers me the possibility of contributing not only to the growth of the literature but to the shaping of the culture as I should like it to be." Despite criticism from younger blacks who argued that he did not present a true picture of the plight of black Americans, Ellison remained firm on his stance, insisting that the struggles of blacks, although different in some respects from the struggles of whites, were basically the same struggles all Americans had to face in order to achieve a sense of personal freedom and responsibility.

Commenting on Blacks in America

According to Ellison, "[One writes] out of one thing only—one's experience as understood through one's knowledge of self, culture, and literature." His dedication to this concept is evident in his writings, which focus on the struggles of black Americans striving to be accepted as simply Americans.

Renowned author and critic Henry Louis Gates Jr. once wrote that Ellison, Richard Wright (1908–60) and James Baldwin (1924–87) comprised "the holy male trinity of the black tradition." Wright, most famous for his protest novel *Native Son*, was known for depicting blacks as oppressed victims of white society, and Baldwin—best known for his nonfiction works such as *Notes of a Native Son*, *Nobody Knows My Name*, and *The Fire Next Time*—focused on religious themes and "blackness as salvation." But only Ellison, who saw blackness as a metaphor for the human condition, transcended the theme of race by incorporating mythological and supernatural elements into his works. Thus, while *Invisible Man* explores the narrator's attempt to cope with racism and segregation, it also explores one man's attempts to come to terms with the myth of the American Dream and to make sense of a society in which both the oppressed and the oppressor become victims of their blindness concerning American identity and the true brotherhood of humanity. Consequently, Ellison is renowned not only as an author and the master of black vernacular, but as an astute commentator on literature, culture, and race.

INTRODUCTION TO THE NOVEL

Introduction 8

A Brief Synopsis 11

List of Characters 13

Character Map 19

Introduction

"In our society, it is not unusual for a Negro to experience a sensation that he does not exist in the real world at all. He seems rather to exist in the nightmarish fantasy of the white American mind as a phantom that the white mind seeks unceasingly, by means both crude and subtle, to lay." ("An American Dilemma: A Review," *Shadow and Act*)

This quote from Ralph Ellison's review of Swedish sociologist Gunnar Myrdal's book *An American Dilemma* (which explores the roots of prejudice and racism in the U.S.) anticipates the premise of *Invisible Man*: Racism is a devastating force, possessing the power to render black Americans virtually invisible.

Hailed as a novel that "changed the shape of American literature," *Invisible Man* traces the nightmarish journey of its unnamed narrator from his high school and college days in the South to his harrowing experiences in the North as a member of the Brotherhood, a powerful organization that purports to fight for justice and equality for all people but in reality exploits blacks and uses them to promote its own political agenda. By describing one man's lifelong struggle to establish a sense of identity as a black man in white America, Ellison illustrates the powerful social and political forces that conspire to keep black Americans "in their place," denying them the "inalienable right to life, liberty, and the pursuit of happiness" guaranteed to all Americans. (As numerous historians have pointed out, the U.S. Constitution explicitly excludes black Americans, who, until 1865, were perceived not as men, but as property.)

Often described as a *bildungsroman*, or coming-of-age story, *Invisible Man* is the tale of a black man's search for identity and visibility in white America. Convinced that his existence depends on gaining the support, recognition, and approval of whites—whom he has been taught to view as powerful, *superior* beings who control his destiny— the narrator spends nearly 20 years trying to establish his humanity in a society that refuses to see him as a human being. Ultimately, he realizes that he must create his own identity, which rests not on the acceptance of whites, but on his own acceptance of the past. Although *Invisible Man* received the prestigious National Book Award, some blacks feel that the novel perpetuates black stereotypes. In addition, some black scholars criticized the novel for not being sufficiently "revolutionary" and not accurately depicting "the black experience." Ellison's attitude towards these critics is perhaps best summarized in his classic response to a reporter during a 1973 interview: "I'll be my kind of militant." Black feminists also criticized the novel, pointing to the lack of positive female characters, and noting that the women in the novel are all prostitutes, sex objects, or caregivers. Despite these criticisms, Ellison's novel, regarded as a classic of American literature, enjoyed immense popularity.

Published in 1952, more than a decade before the Civil Rights Act of 1964 declared racial segregation illegal, *Invisible Man* has been praised for its innovative style and unique treatment of controversial subject matter. The violence and racial tension depicted in *Invisible Man* foreshadow the violence engendered by the Civil Rights Movement in cities across the U.S. The action of *Invisible Man* spans approximately 20 years, tracing the narrator's life from his high school graduation in Greenwood, South Carolina, to his involvement in the Harlem Riot of 1943. By tracing the narrator's journey from the rural South to the urban North, the novel emulates the movement of the *slave narratives*, autobiographies written by formerly enslaved black Africans that trace their escape routes from bondage in the South to freedom in the North. One of the most famous slave narratives is Frederick Douglass' autobiography, *Narrative of the Life of Frederick Douglass, an American Slave*, published in 1845. This fact is important to our understanding of *Invisible Man*, because Frederick Douglass (like the narrator's grandfather) symbolizes the *ghost* of slavery alluded to at several critical points in the novel.

The narrator's path also traces the path of thousands of Southern blacks who moved to the North during the 1930s and 40s in search of better jobs and new opportunities during the Great Migration.

Call and response—a concept rooted in the traditional Negro sermons in which the pastor's impassioned *call* elicits an equally impassioned *response* from the congregation—is one of the defining elements of African American literature. With this in mind, *Invisible Man* can be read as a response to Langston Hughes' poem, "Harlem," which poses the question, "What happens to a dream deferred? . . . Does it explode?" According to Ellison, who also explores the myth of the American Dream, the answer is a resounding, "Yes!" In addition to Langston Hughes, the two authors who had the greatest influence on Ellison's writing style were T. S. Eliot and Richard Wright. Ellison was especially intrigued with Eliot's *Wasteland*, a poem that explores the spiritual wasteland of contemporary society, and with Wright's acclaimed protest novel, *Native Son*, and his nonfiction work,

12 Million Black Voices, which Ellison felt was even more powerful than *Native Son*. Ellison was also influenced by H.G. Wells' science fiction novel, *The Invisible Man*, and Richard Wright's short story, "The Man Who Lived Underground."

A complex, multi-layered novel, *Invisible Man* can be read as an *allegory* (a story with both a literal and symbolic meaning that can be read, understood, and interpreted at several levels) that traces the narrator's perilous journey from innocence to experience, and from blind ignorance to enlightened awareness. *Invisible Man* can also be read as a *quest narrative*. Like Homer's *Odyssey* and Dante's *Divine Comedy*—both of which are alluded to in the novel—*Invisible Man* involves a symbolic journey to the underworld, where the narrator must meet and defeat various monsters—such as Brother Jack—and overcome seemingly impossible trials in order to return home.

Ellison's use of *inverted reality*, creating a world that mirrors the reality of the white world, is a key structural element in *Invisible Man*. In the narrator's world, black is white, up is down, light is darkness, and insanity is sanity. This structural device is used to illustrate that blacks, due to their perceived *inferior* status in American society, often experience a radically different reality than whites, creating the illusion that blacks and whites live in two different worlds. The white man's American dream is the black man's nightmare, and behavior deemed normal for whites is deemed abnormal (or crazy) for blacks. A key example is the novel's closing scene: The narrator returns to his underground home, the basement (coal cellar) of a whites-only apartment building. Although this can be viewed as a physical move *down* into darkness and despair, in the narrator's inverted reality, his return to his underground habitat illustrates a psychological move *up* towards awareness and enlightenment.

Unlike conventional novels that present a series of related sequential events, *Invisible Man* consists of a series of seemingly unrelated scenes or episodes—often expressed in the form of stories or sermons—linked only by the narrator's comments and observations. In this way, the structure of the novel mirrors the structure of a jazz composition, players stepping forward to perform their impromptu solos, then stepping back to rejoin their group.

The structure also emulates the *oral tradition* of preliterate societies. Passed down orally from generation to generation, their stories embodied a people's culture and history. In the novel, each character's story can be viewed as a lesson that contributes to the narrator's growth and awareness, bringing him closer to an understanding of his own people's culture and history.

A Brief Synopsis

Invisible Man is the story of a young, college-educated black man struggling to survive and succeed in a racially divided society that refuses to see him as a human being. Told in the form of a first-person narrative, *Invisible Man* traces the nameless narrator's physical and psychological journey from blind ignorance to enlightened awareness—or, according to the author, "from Purpose to Passion to Perception"—through a series of flashbacks in the forms of dreams and memories. Set in the U.S. during the pre–Civil Rights era when segregation laws barred black Americans from enjoying the same basic human rights as their white counterparts, the novel opens in the South (Greenwood, South Carolina), although the majority of the action takes place in the North (Harlem, New York).

In the Prologue, the narrator—speaking to us from his underground hideout in the basement (coal cellar) of a whites-only apartment building—reminisces about his life as an invisible man. Now in his 40s, he recalls a time when he was a naïve young man, eager to become a renowned educator and orator. The narrator begins his story by recalling his high school graduation speech, which attracted the attention of the white school superintendent who invites him to give the same speech at a local hotel to the town's leading white citizens. But when he arrives at the hotel, the narrator is forced to participate in a brutal blindfolded boxing match (the "battle royal") with nine of his classmates, an event, which, he discovers, is part of the evening's entertainment for the "smoker" (a kind of stag party). The entertainment also includes a sensuous dance by a naked blonde woman, and the boys are forced to watch. The boxing match is followed by a humiliating event: The boys must scramble for what appear to be gold coins on an electrified rug (but, which turn out to be only worthless brass tokens). Then the narrator—now bruised and bleeding—is finally allowed to give his speech in front of the drunken white men who largely ignore him until he accidentally uses the phrase "social equality" instead of "social responsibility" to describe the role of blacks in America. At the end of his speech—despite his degrading and humiliating ordeal—the narrator proudly accepts his prize: a calfskin briefcase containing a scholarship to the state college for Negroes.

That night, the narrator's dead grandfather—a former slave—appears in a dream, ordering him to open the briefcase and look inside. Instead of the scholarship, the briefcase contains a note that reads, "Keep This Nigger Boy Running." The dream sets the stage. For the next 20 years of his life, the narrator stumbles blindly through life, never stopping to question why he is always kept running by people—both black and white—who profess to guide and direct him, but who ultimately exploit him and betray his trust.

Focusing on the events of one fateful day, the narrator then recalls his college days. Assigned to chauffeur Mr. Norton, a prominent white visiting trustee, around the campus, the narrator follows Mr. Norton's orders and takes him to visit two sites in the nearby black neighborhood—the cabin of Jim Trueblood, a local sharecropper, and the Golden Day, a disreputable bar/half-way house for shell-shocked World War I veterans. The narrator, however, is expelled from his beloved college for taking Mr. Norton to these places and sent to New York, armed with seven letters from his dean (Dr. Bledsoe). The letters, he believed, are letters of recommendation, but are in reality letters confirming his expulsion.

Arriving in New York City, the narrator is amazed by what he perceives to be unlimited freedom for blacks. He is especially intrigued by a black West Indian man (later identified as Ras the Exhorter) whom he first encounters addressing a group of men and women on the streets of Harlem, urging them to work together to unite their black community. But the narrator's excitement soon turns to disillusionment as he discovers that the North presents the same barriers to black achievement as the South.

Realizing that he cannot return to college, the narrator accepts a job at a paint factory famous for its optic white paint, unaware that he is one of several blacks hired to replace white workers out on strike. Nearly killed in a factory explosion, the narrator subsequently undergoes a grueling ordeal at the paint factory hospital, where he finds himself the object of a strange experiment by the hospital's white doctors.

Following his release from the hospital, the narrator finds refuge in the home of Mary Rambo, a kind and generous black woman, who feeds him and nurses him back to health. Although grateful to Mary, whom he acknowledges as his only friend, the narrator—anxious to earn a living and *do something* with his life—eventually leaves Mary to join the Brotherhood, a political organization that professes to be dedicated to achieving equality for all people. Under the guidance of the Brotherhood and its leader, Brother Jack, the narrator becomes an accomplished speaker and leader of the Harlem District. He also has an abortive liaison with Sybil, a sexually frustrated white woman who sees him as the embodiment of the stereotypical black man endowed with extraordinary sexual prowess.

But after the tragic death of his friend Tod Clifton, a charismatic young black "Brother" who is shot by a white policeman, the narrator becomes disillusioned with the disparity between what the organization preaches and what its leaders practice. As a result, he decides to leave the Brotherhood, headquartered in an affluent section of Manhattan, and returns to Harlem where he is confronted by Ras the Exhorter (now Ras the Destroyer) who accuses him of betraying the black community. To escape the wrath of Ras and his men, the narrator disguises himself by donning a hat and dark glasses. In disguise, he is repeatedly mistaken for someone named Rinehart, a con man who uses his *invisibility* to his own advantage.

The narrator discovers that the Harlem community has erupted in violence. Eager to demonstrate that he is no longer part of the Brotherhood, the narrator allows himself to be drawn into the violence and chaos of the Harlem riot and participates in the burning of a Harlem tenement. Later, as he flees the scene of the burning building and tries to find his way back to Mary's, two white men with baseball bats pursue him. To escape his assailants, he leaps into a manhole, which lands him in his underground hideout.

For the next several days the sick and delusional narrator suffers horrific nightmares in which he is captured and castrated by a group of men led by Brother Jack. Finally able to let go of his painful past—symbolized by the various items in his briefcase—the narrator discovers that writing down his experiences enables him to release his hatred and rediscover his love of life.

List of Characters

Invisible Man features a long and complex cast of colorful characters the narrator meets on his quest for meaning and identity who function on both a literal and symbolic level. Many are simply ordinary, everyday people living ordinary, everyday lives. Because their significance depends solely on how the narrator chooses to see them, none can be clearly designated as major or minor characters.

Following are brief descriptions of the key characters, listed in order of their appearance in the novel.

The South (Greenwood, South Carolina)

The narrator (the "Invisible Man")   A misguided, miseducated young man whose quest for meaning and identity as a black man in white America leads him into numerous dangerous situations. Although he undoubtedly has a name, he remains nameless and "invisible" throughout the novel.

The grandfather   The narrator's ancestor and spiritual guide whose deathbed revelation haunts the narrator throughout the novel and serves as a catalyst for his quest. He appears in the novel only through the narrator's memories.

The school superintendent   The nameless white man who invites the narrator to give his high school graduation speech at the smoker, where he acts as master of ceremonies. After tricking him into participating in the battle royal, he rewards him with a calfskin briefcase and "a scholarship to the state college for Negroes."

Jackson   The most brutal, sadistic white man at the battle royal. Jackson's overt racism and vicious—albeit thwarted—attack on the narrator foreshadows Brother Jack's covert racism and equally vicious attack on the narrator's psyche.

Tatlock   The largest of the ten black boys forced to participate in the battle royal. Tatlock and the narrator are final contestants in the bloody boxing match, which results in a temporary deadlock. In the end, Tatlock defeats the narrator and proudly accepts his $10 prize.

Mr. Norton   A white Northern liberal and multi-millionaire who provides financial support for Dr. Bledsoe's college. A "smoker of cigars [and] teller of polite Negro stories," Mr. Norton is a covert racist who hides his true feelings behind a mask of philanthropy.

The Founder Modeled after Booker T. Washington, founder of Alabama's Tuskegee Institute, the Founder exemplifies the black American who rose "up from slavery" to achieve the American Dream. Although he does not appear in the novel, the Founder (like the grandfather) exerts a powerful influence on the narrator.

Dr. A. Hebert Bledsoe Known to his students as "Old Bucket-head" because of his fondness for reciting the Founder's famous speech on service and humility ("Cast Down Your Bucket"), Dr. Bledsoe is the president of the black college established by the Founder. Entrusted to fulfill the legacy of the Founder's dream, Dr. Bledsoe destroys the dream to promote his own selfish interests.

Rev. Homer A. Barbee The blind Southern preacher from Chicago who visits the campus to deliver a moving sermon about the Founder's life and death. Like his namesake (the blind poet Homer, author of *The Odyssey* and *The Iliad*), Reverend Barbee is a powerful orator and storyteller.

Jim Trueblood Although readers may tend to think of him primarily as the sharecropper who has sex with his teenage daughter, Jim Trueblood is the only true "brother" ("blood") in the novel: He accepts full responsibility for his behavior, makes peace with his God, and fights for himself, his family, and his land.

Kate and Matty Lou Jim Trueblood's wife and daughter, respectively.

Mr. and Mrs. Broadnax (Broad-in-Acts) The white couple who appear in Jim Trueblood's dream. Mr. Broadnax, like Mr. Norton, is a racist who hides behind a mask of philanthropy.

The vet One of the shellshocked veterans at the Golden Day tavern. Because of his candid speech, his brutal honesty, and his refusal to act subservient toward whites, he is considered dangerous and hastily transferred to St. Elizabeth's Hospital, a mental institution in Washington, D.C.

Supercargo   The warden/attendant who transports the veterans from the hospital to the Golden Day once a week. The veterans hate him because he represents the white power structure.

Big Halley   The bartender at the Golden Day. Although Supercargo is officially charged with keeping order at the Golden Day, it is Big Halley who ultimately maintains control. He has his finger on the pulse of the black community.

Burnside and Sylvester   Veterans at the Golden Day. Burnside is a former doctor. Sylvester leads the vicious attack on Supercargo.

Edna, Hester, and Charlene   Black prostitutes at the Golden Day. Edna harbors sexual fantasies about white men and playfully propositions Mr. Norton.

Crenshaw   The attendant who accompanies the vet to St. Elizabeth's Hospital.

The North (Harlem and Manhattan, New York)

Ras the Exhorter (later Ras the Destroyer)   Modeled after renowned black leader Marcus Garvey, Ras is a powerful orator and black nationalist leader who believes that integration with whites is impossible. He is violently opposed to the Brotherhood.

Young Mr. Emerson   Mr. Emerson's presumably homosexual son. Because he himself is alienated from society, young Emerson empathizes with the narrator and shows him the contents of Dr. Bledsoe's letter, addressed to his father. He also tells him about the job opening at the Liberty Paint Factory.

Mr. MacDuffy   Personnel manager at the Liberty Paint Factory who hires the narrator as one of several blacks chosen to replace white union workers out on strike.

Mr. Kimbro   Superintendent at the Liberty Paint Factory, known to his employees as "the Colonel" and "slave driver."

Lucius Brockway   The black man in charge of mixing paints and regulating the pressure on the boilers in the basement of the Liberty Paint Factory. Terrified of losing his job, Brockway causes the explosion that lands the narrator in the factory hospital. Like Dr. Bledsoe, Brockway is a "gatekeeper" who jealously guards his position and does his best to keep other blacks—whom he views as potential competitors for his job—out of the company.

Mary Rambo   The kindly, black Southern woman who cares for the narrator after his release from the factory hospital. Although she lives in Harlem, Mary refused to let the corruption of the big city destroy her spirit.

Sister and Brother Provo   The elderly couple evicted from their Harlem apartment.

Brother Jack   Leader of the Brotherhood, a powerful political organization that professes to defend the rights of the poor. He invites the narrator to join the Brotherhood and sets him up as spokesman of the Harlem District, then expels him for being "an opportunist."

Brother Hambro   The white brother who trains the narrator in the art of scientific rhetoric.

Brother Tod Clifton   The handsome, charismatic young black brother assigned as Harlem's Youth Leader. Noted for his commitment to black youth, his idealism, and his Afro-Anglo-Saxon features, Brother Clifton is killed by a white policeman who arrests him for selling Sambo dolls on a Harlem street corner.

Brother Tarp   An elderly black man who spent nineteen years in prison for saying "No" to a white man. He gives the narrator a link from the iron chain he was forced to wear on his leg as a prisoner and portrait of Frederick Douglass for his office.

Brother Tobitt   A white brother married to a black woman who believes his marital relationship provides him with special insight into the psychology of black people.

Brother Wrestrum   The brother who tries to wrest power from the narrator by accusing him of being an opportunist. He finally succeeds in getting him transferred out of the Harlem district.

Brother Maceo   The missing brother whom the narrator eventually meets at the Jolly Dollar, a Harlem bar and grill.

Brother Garnett   The white brother who half-heartedly supports the narrator following his accusation by Brother Wrestrum.

Brother MacAfee   The brother who appears to empathize with the narrator, but points out that his actions have endangered the Brotherhood.

Emma   A shrewd, intelligent, sophisticated woman who revels in her power as Brother Jack's mistress. Although sexually attracted to the narrator, she realizes that getting involved with him could cause her to lose her favored position.

Hubert's Wife   The nameless white woman with whom the narrator has a brief sexual encounter.

Sybil   The wife of another Brotherhood member (George). Sybil has rape fantasies involving black men and tries to seduce the narrator.

Dupre and Scofield   Looters/leaders of the Harlem Riot, duped into believing that violence and destruction are the answers to racism and hatred.

B. P. Rinehart   A master of disguise who creates his own identity. Among the residents of the Harlem community, he is known as a preacher ("spiritual technologist"), a lover, a numbers runner, and a pimp.

Character Map

Although he appears only in the narrator's dreams and memories, the grandfather—who represents "the ancestor" or the ghost of slavery—is one of the most prominent figures in the novel. Equally important is Rinehart who, by representing the "rind" and "heart" of humanity, shows the narrator how to become his own man, thus offering him hope for the future.

Many of the people the narrator encounters in the North appear to be mirror images of people he encountered in the South. The following chart illustrates these relationships.

The Grandfather
("The Ancestor")
Represents the past and
the ghost of slavery

The South	Character's Role	The North
The School Superintendent	The White "Liberal"	Brother Jack
Mr. Norton	The Trustee/Benefactor	Mr. Emerson
Dr. Bledsoe	The Sellout/Opportunist ("The Black Powerhouse")	Lucius Brockway
Jim Trueblood	The True "Brother"	Brother Tarp
Rev. Barbee	The Orator	Ras the Exhorter
Big Halley (The Golden Day)	The Bartender	Barrelhouse (The Jolly Dollar)
The Naked Blonde	The "Taboo" White Woman	Sybil
The Narrator's Mother	The Mother/Caretaker	Mary Rambo
The Narrator	The Prizefighter	Brother Tod Clifton

Rinehart
("The Trickster")
Represents a new
survival strategy
for the future

CRITICAL COMMENTARIES

Prologue 22

Chapter 1 26

Chapter 2 30

Chapters 3–4 34

Chapters 5–6 39

Chapters 7–9 43

Chapters 10–12 48

Chapter 13 52

Chapters 14–16 55

Chapter 17 60

Chapters 18–19 64

Chapters 20–21 67

Chapter 22 71

Chapter 23 74

Chapter 24 77

Chapter 25 80

Epilogue 84

Prologue

Summary

Without giving a name, the narrator introduces himself as a man, not a ghost, describing the nature of his invisibility: People refuse to see him. Although he considered his invisibility a disadvantage, he points out that it has become an asset. To illustrate, the narrator relates an incident in which he almost killed a white man in the street for insulting him until he realized the absurdity of a sleepwalker being killed by a phantom, existing only in the white man's nightmares. Besides, because he is invisible, the narrator is able to live rent-free and avail himself of free electricity.

Describing his underground home: the coal cellar of a whites-only building "in a section of the basement that was shut off and forgotten during the nineteenth century," the narrator avoids the picture of a dark hole or crypt, hastening to explain that his cellar is illuminated by 1,369 light bulbs.

The narrator, a music lover, has only one radio-phonograph but plans to have five so that he can feel as well as hear his music. He imagines what it would feel like to have five recordings of Louis Armstrong's "What Did I Do to Be So Black and Blue" playing simultaneously. The narrator's thoughts on music lead him to reminisce about a time he listened to music while smoking a reefer (marijuana joint), amazed at his ability to descend into "breaks" within the music, which normally seemed like one continuous flow. He compares his experience interrupting the flow of time to a prizefight in which the champion was beaten by a yokel (amateur) simply because the latter interrupted his opponent's timing.

Next, while listening to Louis Armstrong's music, the narrator describes several visions, which seem to merge into one extended vision, including a woman standing on an auction block as a group of slave owners bid for her naked body; a man delivering a sermon on "The Blackness of Blackness"; and an old black woman pleading for freedom, who tells the narrator that she killed her white husband/master to save him from the hatred of his two mulatto sons.

Commentary

A Prologue generally consists of an opening speech or introduction to a literary work. Here, the Prologue anticipates the Epilogue. Together, these two elements frame the novel, which begins and ends in chaos.

Obsessed with a need for light to validate his existence, after 20 years seeking his true identity the narrator finally understands the difference between seeing through "physical eyes" and perceiving reality through one's "inner eyes" (that is, he is no longer "blind"). Discovering how to turn his invisibility into an asset because no one acknowledges his existence, the narrator realizes he can live rent-free and obtain enough free electricity from Monopolated Light & Power (the white power source) to fill his "hole" with light. In fact, he points out that his "hole" is illuminated by 1,369 light bulbs. This number may seem like merely a descriptive detail, but 1936—the year Ellison arrived in New York City and met Alain Locke and Langston Hughes—becomes 1,369 by simply switching two digits, revealing yet another example of Ellison's use of number symbolism. Ellison's numeric "joke" also illustrates his knack for merging elements of fact and fiction.

Keeping in mind that Ellison's story is an allegory, the narrator's focus on light, light bulbs, and illumination can be interpreted as referring to the process of intellectual enlightenment, and the narrator's seemingly random comments begin to make sense. Through the narrator's numerous references to fighting, Ellison introduces the prizefight imagery in Chapter 1 with the battle royal, playing a key role throughout the novel.

This scene also introduces the concept of fate, illustrating that despite our scientific knowledge and our diligent efforts to prepare ourselves to meet life's challenges, some things are simply beyond our control.

The narrator's discussion of Louis Armstrong's "What Did I Do to Be So Black and Blue?" introduces a theme that resonates throughout the novel: the power of music, often helping the narrator transcend reality and mentally retreat to another place and time. The music theme is underscored by numerous references to musical works, terms, and instruments, including references to blaring trumpets, hectic rhythms, and "a tom-tom beating like heart-thuds." The Prologue also introduces Ellison's color symbolism, as indicated by numerous references to black and white (ivory), and red, white, and blue.

Numerous references to "stepping outside of time" and "interrupting the flow" of time as well as the description of history as moving "not like an arrow but a boomerang," introduces another important insight regarding time and history: that, like the flight of a boomerang, history travels in a circular path and always returns to its origins. As the narrator points out, "the end is in the beginning."

References to "bodiless heads . . . in circus sideshows" and the funhouse where people find themselves "surrounded by mirrors of hard, distorting glass" create a striking circus metaphor that Ellison carries throughout the novel. Trained animal performances and freaks of nature—the two-headed man, the bearded lady, and so forth—are so far removed from the normal world that onlookers find it inconceivable to identify with them on a human level. By establishing this premise in a novel about a black man's search for identity, Ellison underscores the racial rift that separates blacks and whites not because they are inherently different, but because whites refuse to see blacks as fully human.

Invisible Man's humor, irony, and satire, as well as the narrator's fondness for wordplay, reveal Ellison's sensitivity to the nuances of the English language. The Prologue's references to "the master meter," the "power station," and "free current" all relate to the underlying themes of power, freedom, and the legacy of slavery. Intertwined with these concepts are images of hell and "the jungle of Harlem." Similarly, the narrator's insistence on precise definitions of terms and concepts (freedom, hibernation, responsibility, and invisibility) illustrates his awareness of the power of language.

In the Prologue, Ellison also prepares us for the numerous allusions to classic works of fiction, nonfiction, and folklore that appear throughout the novel, at times merging elements of fiction and folklore. The narrator's statement, "Call me Jack-the-Bear" alludes to the opening line of Herman Melville's *Moby Dick*, "Call me Ishmael." It also alludes to the Br'er Rabbit folktales based on African folklore, featuring characters such as Jack-the-Bear, Br'er Fox, and Br'er Rabbit.

Glossary

(Here and in the following chapters, difficult words and phrases, as well as allusions and historical references, are explained.)

Edgar Allan Poe American poet, short-story writer, and critic (1809–1849), best known for his tales of horror.

ectoplasm   the vaporous, luminous substance believed by spiritualists to emanate from a medium in a trance.

epidermis   the outermost layer of the skin.

bilious   having or resulting from some ailment of the bile or the liver.

Louis Armstrong   American jazz musician (1901–71). Lauded as the world's greatest trumpet player, Armstrong was noted for his unique impact on the history of jazz due to his technical skill in trumpet playing and his innovative style of "scat" singing.

Dante   allusion to Dante Alighieri, author of *The Divine Comedy*, a classic work that traces the soul's journey through the underworld towards divine enlightenment.

Weltschmerz   German for "world pain"; sentimental pessimism or melancholy over the state of the world.

flamenco   Spanish gypsy style of dance (characterized by stomping, clapping) or music (typically very emotional and mournful).

I might forget to dodge some bright morning   allusion to Richard Wright's short story, "Bright and Morning Star," about a mother and son who are brutally murdered after being betrayed by a white "comrade."

All sickness is not unto death   allusion to Soren Kierkegaard (1813–55), a Danish philosopher noted for his philosophy of Existentialism. Kierkegaard is the author of *The Sickness Unto Death: A Christian Exposition for Edification and Awakening*, which contends that the "sickness unto death" is despair.

Chapter 1

Summary

The narrator—speaking in the voice of a man in his 40s—reminiscing about his youth, opens the novel. He remembers when he had not yet discovered his identity or realized that he was an invisible man. The narrator relates an anecdote concerning his grandfather who, on his deathbed, shocks his family by revealing himself as a traitor and a spy (to his race). The narrator also recalls being invited to give his high school graduation speech at a gathering of the town's leading white citizens. When he arrived, he discovered that he was to provide part of the evening's entertainment for a roomful of drunken white men as a contestant, along with nine of his classmates, in a blindfolded boxing match (a "battle royal") before giving his speech. The entertainment includes an erotic dance by a naked blonde woman with a flag tattoo on her stomach, which he and his classmates are forced to watch. After enduring these humiliating experiences, the narrator is finally permitted to give his speech and receives his prize: a calfskin briefcase that contains a scholarship to the local college for Negroes (a term Ellison preferred over "blacks").

That night, the narrator dreams that he is at the circus with his grandfather, who refuses to laugh at the clowns. His grandfather orders him to open the briefcase and read the message contained in an official envelope stamped with the state seal. Opening the envelope, the narrator finds that each envelope contains yet another envelope. In the last envelope, instead of the scholarship, he finds an engraved document with the message: "To Whom It May Concern: Keep This Nigger-Boy Running."

Commentary

Chapter 1 consists of six key episodes: (1) the grandfather's deathbed scene, (2) the narrator's arrival at the hotel, (3) the naked blonde's erotic dance, (4) the battle royal, (5) the narrator's speech, and (6) the narrator's dream.

(1) The grandfather's deathbed scene. Although it may appear merely incidental, this episode is an integral part of the novel because the grandfather, representing the ancestor or ghost of slavery, has a major impact on the narrator's life. Determined to rid himself of the past, the narrator is nevertheless compelled to come to terms with his past before he can handle his present and future.

During the course of the novel, the grandfather's spirit appears to the narrator on several occasions, providing his grandson with spiritual guidance, representing the legacy of slavery that continues to haunt black Americans, regardless of their social, political, or economic progress.

(2) The narrator's arrival at the hotel. This episode introduces betrayal, broken promises, and game-playing themes. Although as a young high school graduate he naïvely assumed he had some choice in whether to participate in the battle royal, looking back on the incident, he realizes that he had no choice. The only way he would be granted the opportunity to give his speech was to first participate in the humiliating blindfolded boxing match. The book contains many other instances in which the narrator experiences a sense of betrayal as he is forced to abide by arbitrary rules devised by others.

(3) The naked blonde's erotic dance. Overall, this scene represents America's distorted value system. The American dream of freedom, liberty, and equality (symbolized by the flag tattoo) has been replaced by the relentless pursuit of money, sex, and power (symbolized by the car advertising tokens).

Introducing the imagery of people as dolls and puppets, the narrator describes the blonde as having yellow hair "like . . . a circus Kewpie doll." Later, a blow to the narrator's head causes his right eye to pop "like a jack-in-the-box." Ellison describes people as dolls or puppets elsewhere in the book, an image that emphasizes powerlessness.

(4) The battle royal. The battle royal is a brutal rite of passage that thrusts the naïve narrator into a violent, chaotic world where the rules that govern a society do not apply (there are "no rounds [and] no bells at three-minute intervals"). By participating in the battle royal, the narrator learns that life is a struggle for survival, but at this point he still believes in the philosophy of Booker T. Washington: that blacks can achieve success through education and industry. Symbolically, the scene introduces the theme of struggle among blacks for an elusive prize that often remains out of reach.

Theme

The battle royal symbolizes the social and political power struggle depicted throughout the novel. Central to this struggle are the issues of race, class, and gender, three concepts the narrator must come to terms with before he can acknowledge and accept his identity as a black man in white America. To underscore his message that blacks forced to live in a segregated society are denied their human rights, Ellison uses two powerful symbolic elements: the white blindfolds and the brass tokens.

The white blindfolds symbolize the narrator's being "blinded by the white." Inundated by white racist propaganda concerning the inferiority of blacks, the narrator begins to internalize these destructive messages, no longer seeing the truth. Made of brass, an alloy of copper and zinc, the tokens consist of a combination of two pure elements, symbolizing the role of black Americans, who represent a blend of African and American/black and white cultures. Because none of the boys can afford to buy the cars advertised, the tokens underscore the economic inequity between blacks and whites. The tokens also suggest the worthless, empty gesture inherent in tokenism—the practice of including a select few blacks into white society without granting all blacks social equality as well as social responsibility.

(5) The narrator's speech. The narrator's speech introduces a pattern of irony and duality that pervades the novel. While the narrator professes to disagree with Booker T. Washington's views on race relations, he presents Washington's conciliatory 1895 Atlanta Exposition address, urging blacks to be patient and accept "social responsibility" without "social equality," at his high school graduation. In doing so, he establishes a pattern of simply doing what others expect of him, without examining his motives, establishing his own value system, or considering the consequences of his actions. Evidenced in subsequent chapters, the narrator's tendency to act without thinking and to accept others' judgments without question keeps him from discovering his true identity.

Style & Language

The calfskin briefcase highlights the emphasis on skin and underscores the relationship between the fate of the calf and the narrator's potential fate as one who is about to be sacrificed on the altar of racism.

(6) The narrator's dream. The narrator's dream symbolizes the myth of the American Dream, holding that Americans can achieve their dreams, if only they are willing to work hard and pursue their goals. Clearly, the narrator's experience has taught him that this is not true for black Americans.

In addition to the theme of dreams and visions, which plays a key role throughout the novel, the narrator's dream also introduces the theme of the running man, alluded to in the phrase, "Keep this Nigger-Boy Running." The running-man theme is a major motif in African American literature, tracing its roots to the slave narrative. But unlike enslaved Africans, often forced to run for their lives, the narrator starts running and is kept running by others who seem to have little real impact on his life. The narrator is on the run throughout the novel.

Music, the language of music, as well as musical sounds and rhythms, pervade and provide the narrative framework for the novel, structured like a jazz composition. The sensuous music of a clarinet provides the accompaniment for the blonde's dance and the background for the battle royal. Conveying the novel's color imagery, white men with blue eyes and red faces and the naked blonde's white skin, red lips, and blue eyes *color* these scenes all-American, part of a red, white, and blue color motif.

Glossary

smoker   an informal social gathering for men only.

rococo   a style of architecture, decorative art, music, etc., of the early eighteenth century developed from and in reaction to the Baroque and characterized by profuse and delicate ornamentation, reduced scale, lightness, grace, etc.

Kewpie doll   from Cupid; trademark for a chubby, rosy-faced doll with its hair in a topknot.

Chapter 2

Summary

As the chapter opens, the narrator is a student at the black college to which he received a scholarship. Continuing his quest for acceptance and identity, and eager to impress Mr. Norton, a visiting white trustee, the narrator chauffeurs Mr. Norton to the old slave quarters on the outskirts of the campus. Along the way, Mr. Norton tells him about his dead daughter. As the narrator drives by Jim Trueblood's log cabin, Mr. Norton orders him to stop the car so that he can talk to Trueblood. Horrified, fascinated, and mesmerized, Norton listens to the sharecropper's story of his incestuous encounter with his daughter, Matty Lou. Before departing, Norton gives Trueblood a hundred-dollar bill, then instructs the narrator to get him some whiskey to calm his nerves. Deciding that downtown is too far to go, the narrator heads for the Golden Day, a local black bar with a dubious reputation.

Commentary

Raising several critical issues concerning love, family loyalty, mortal sin, and morality, this chapter explores the concept of *moral absolutes*: Are certain acts morally wrong, regardless of circumstances, or are there shades of right and wrong? Finally, the text addresses the complex themes of black sexuality and manhood. Trueblood's story is central to all these issues.

Through Trueblood, Ellison explores our all-too-human tendency to judge an individual on the basis of a single, isolated act. Trueblood's behavior before and after the incident with his daughter characterizes him as an intelligent, hard-working, loving man. Despite his extreme poverty, Trueblood is the only man in the entire novel—black or white—who has a family and provides for them to the best of his ability.

Mr. Norton's one-hundred-dollar reward indicates that Norton is no different from the other white men who have exploited Trueblood's pain for their own vicarious pleasure. Norton, whom the narrator describes as a "Bostonian, smoker of cigars" has much in common with the men at the smoker and with Mr. and Mrs. Broadnax (Broad-in-acts), philanthropists who make a public display of helping blacks while referring to them as "niggers."

Ironically, the narrator, who experienced the same type of treatment at the hands of the men at the smoker, is totally oblivious to Trueblood's situation. Instead of empathizing with him or being sympathetic to his pain, the narrator dismisses Trueblood as a brutal, animalistic creature. The narrator also fears that Trueblood's behavior might convince Mr. Norton to think less of him. Consequently, he is eager to get back to the campus so that Norton can see "civilized," educated blacks, hoping Norton will forget about Trueblood.

Literary Device

By comparing Trueblood and Norton, Ellison explores two cultural myths that are equally false. Just as Norton sees Trueblood as an incarnation of the sexually insatiable *black buck*, the narrator (and Trueblood himself) sees Norton as the incarnation of Santa Claus, the benevolent, paternalistic white man who bestows gifts on children to reward them for good behavior. But Norton, representing a perversion of the Santa Claus myth, rewards his *children* for bad behavior. Similarly, Trueblood, who would undoubtedly be condemned for his behavior if he were white, is instead rewarded for reinforcing and perpetuating the white stereotype of blacks as sexual animals who must be segregated from "civilized" (white) society, and especially from white women.

The process Ellison uses to transform these myths warrants our close attention. First, he *explores* the myths of the jolly, generous Santa Claus and the sexually insatiable black stud—tracing their origins to white, Eurocentric culture—through the characters of Norton and Trueblood. Then, Ellison *transcends* these myths by separating the illusion from the reality. Finally he *transforms* them to conform to the reality of Southern blacks, thereby enabling us to see the myths from a black, Afrocentric perspective. By debunking both myths, Ellison not only encourages a search for the truth behind the myth; he also asks the reader to consider the potentially dangerous, destructive impact of cultural myths.

Character Insight

Trueblood understands his perceived mythical role in the white community, but sacrifices himself in order to protect his family. Fully aware of the game, he decides to *play the nigger* to get his prize: a chance to stay on his land and provide for his family. Trueblood stays true to his blood (family) and emerges not as slave or *Nigger Jim*, (a character in Mark Twain's *Huckleberry Finn*), but as a humane, compassionate human being who fights the system and wins.

Trueblood's situation raises the issue of moral absolutes. Although Trueblood's behavior cannot be condoned or dismissed, considered within another context, the reader learns that the reason Trueblood's daughter shared a bed with him and his wife in the first place was because the family was trying to survive the bitterly cold winter by huddling together for warmth. Viewed from this perspective, the initial tendency to judge the family's sleeping arrangements as immoral or perverted is reevaluated.

Having dealt with this issue, an analysis of Trueblood's relationship with his wife, Kate, and daughter, Matty Lou, prior to the incident is warranted. Here again, Trueblood was a loving husband and father who provided for his family to the best of his ability. Consequently, Trueblood may be seen as a complex, caring human being, and less likely to be denounced as a monster, based solely on a single (likely unintentional) act committed under highly unusual circumstances.

As in Chapter 1, dreams and illusions play a vital role in defining the character's reality. Like Eliot's Prufrock in "The Love Song of J. Alfred Prufrock," who experiences the sensation of drowning on being awakened by human voices, Trueblood experiences a similar metaphorical death. Awakened by Kate's screams, Trueblood realizes that the woman in his arms is not his wife or his former girlfriend, Margaret, but his own daughter.

Through Trueblood's dream of being trapped inside the clock, Chapter 2 introduces the image of "the man in the machine," which is explored further in subsequent chapters.

Glossary

. . . the bronze statue of the college Founder, . . . his hands outstretched in the breathtaking gesture of lifting the veil allusion to the statue of Booker T. Washington at Tuskegee University (formerly Tuskegee Institute), which depicts Washington lifting the veil off the head of a kneeling slave. Booker Taliaferro Washington (1856–1915), founder of Alabama's Tuskegee Institute, was one of the foremost speakers and educators of the twentieth century. A former slave, Washington believed blacks could achieve success without social equality through education and hard physical labor.

Founder's Day   allusion to the anniversary of the founding of Tuskegee Institute.

Ralph Waldo Emerson   U.S. essayist, philosopher, and poet (1803–82). Emerson is best known for his philosophy of self-reliance. *Invisible Man* author Ralph Waldo Ellison was named after Emerson.

sharecropper   a tenant farmer who works on someone else's land for a share of the crops.

white man's burden   the alleged duty of the white peoples to bring their civilization to other peoples regarded as backward (blacks).

the black-belt people   people living in a region of the Deep South known as the Black Belt because of its large black population.

Chapters 3–4

Summary

Anxious to fulfill Mr. Norton's request for whiskey, the narrator arrives at the Golden Day, a disreputable bar on the outskirts of the college community. Big Halley, the bartender, refuses to let the narrator take a drink outside to Norton. Inside, Norton is propositioned by a prostitute, insulted by a veteran, and overwhelmed by the "inmates"—institutionalized war veterans who fill the bar.

After the narrator and Norton witness the chaotic events at the Golden Day, including the brutal beating of the veteran's attendant, Supercargo, the narrator finally manages to get a distraught Norton—collapsed under the strain of being in a situation where he has no control—back into the car, and the two head back to the college campus.

After dropping Norton off at his rooms, the narrator heads back to the administration building to see Bledsoe. After briefly describing their misadventures and informing Bledsoe that Norton wants to see him, the narrator is shocked and bewildered by Bledsoe's angry outburst that the narrator should have known better than to take Norton to see True-blood's quarters, regardless of his request. Moments later, he is equally shocked as he watches Bledsoe undergo an astounding transformation as he masks his anger and assumes an attitude of conciliation and servility as he prepares to meet with Norton.

On Norton's recommendation, Bledsoe dismisses the narrator and orders him to attend chapel that evening. Back in his room, the narrator is interrupted by a freshman who tells him that Bledsoe wants to see him. Arriving at Bledsoe's office, the narrator is surprised to see Norton, who informs him that Bledsoe had to leave. After apologizing to Norton again, the narrator offers to drive him to the station. Disappointed that his offer is refused, the narrator assures Norton that he intends to read the writings of Ralph Waldo Emerson. This seems to please Norton, who comments on the virtues of Emerson's philosophy of self-reliance, then reminds the narrator about his meeting with Bledsoe. As the narrator leaves, he feels somewhat reassured by Norton, but apprehensive about his impending meeting with Bledsoe and his mandatory attendance at chapel.

Commentary

Chapters 3 and 4 contrast the chaos and violence at the Golden Day with the apparent order and tranquility at the college campus. The two chapters also challenge us to consider what is more *normal*: A bar in which *crazy* people, openly expressing their feelings, dare to challenge a corrupt system that denies them the right to lead dignified, productive lives; or a college that fosters and perpetuates the racist myth of white supremacy, while purporting to prepare its black students to become productive members of society. This quandary is highlighted by the vet's reference to Hester, the prostitute, as "a great humanitarian" whose "healing touch" enables the vets to cope with their broken, empty lives, while the "real" humanitarian—Norton—is likened to "a formless white death."

Literary Device

Symbolizing power, the car is a key element in these chapters. Although the narrator is driving, he is not in control and the car he is driving is not his own. While the narrator exaggerates his importance as Norton's driver, the only power he has is that which Norton bestows on him. Realistically, Norton is in control and the narrator is being *driven* to conform to his expectations. This scene also suggests that the black college controlled by the white trustees is merely an extension of the white power structure.

Furthermore, Bledsoe, under the constant vigilance of his white trustees (represented by Norton), is no more in control of the campus than Big Halley, under the constant surveillance of Supercargo (who also represents the white power structure), is in control of the Golden Day. Big Halley, who resents any outside interference with his bar, in many ways exercises more control than Bledsoe, who willingly accepts the trustees' money and has no qualms about "selling his people."

The chaos at the Golden Day mirrors the confusion at the battle royal. But the roles of the key players have been reversed. At the battle royal, a group of prominent white men drink whiskey and behave like animals. At the Golden Day, black men drink whiskey and behave like animals, as they brutally beat Supercargo and engage in meaningless sex with various prostitutes. At the battle royal, the narrator and his classmates were forced to fight a boxing match while blindfolded. At the Golden Day, the veterans are equally *in the dark* as they try desperately to find some sense of pride and dignity in their wasted, empty lives. In the earlier episode, the narrator arrives at the hotel expecting to give his speech, but is forced to participate in a brutal boxing match instead. Similarly, arriving at the Golden Day, the narrator expects to buy whiskey for Norton, but is relentlessly drawn into the lives of the veterans and forced to witness the brutal attack on Supercargo. In both instances, the narrator's behavior is prompted by his eagerness to please a white man and his belief that if he plays his role well, he will be rewarded.

Theme

These two chapters also advance the theme of reality versus illusion, as things are never quite what they appear to be. Seeing the veterans straggling down the road on the way to the Golden Day, the narrator describes them as looking like a chain gang, although he adds that a chain gang would be walking in a more orderly fashion, thus drawing attention to the veterans' seemingly aimless wanderings. This image of the veterans as prisoners is highlighted again when they are referred to not as patients but "inmates," immediately raising several questions: If these are disabled military veterans, why aren't they in a veterans' hospital? And if they need mental and physical therapy, why are they going to a bar? Although these seem like logical, legitimate questions, Ellison reveals that the veterans are not part of a logical, legitimate society. Although they are indeed war veterans, they are also veterans of the race war. Thus, their wounds are not physical, but psychological. Deprived of the opportunity to practice their skills and forced to live in a segregated society that refuses to reward their accomplishments or acknowledge their achievements, the veterans have social responsibility without social equality.

Literary Device

The Golden Day represents a microcosm of American society from a black perspective, and the shell-shocked veterans represent black men unable to function in the real world as a result of the brutal treatment received at the hands of racist whites.

Here again, Ellison merges fantasy and reality as the vets share their true-to-life stories. Recalling the atrocious behavior towards black World War I veterans, some returned to the States to face extreme hostility for daring to think that their military service earned them the right to equal treatment under the law. The hostilities led to the lynchings of hundreds of African Americans, many of them soldiers still in uniform. The lynchings culminated in the violent Red Summer of 1919, with race riots erupting around the country, especially in major cities such as Detroit and Chicago.

The chapters also provide numerous examples of Ellison's skillful transformation of cultural myths and stereotypes. Edna, the prostitute who fantasizes about Norton's extraordinary sexual prowess, inverts the myth of the black male as sexual stud. Supercargo, the carrier of the black man's burden, transforms Norton's vision of himself as carrying the white man's burden. Supercargo not only literally carries his human cargo—the vets—from the hospital to the Golden Day each week; he also symbolizes the collective psychological burden or *cargo* (guilt, shame, pain, humiliation) of black men, which is why he invokes so much hatred. The scene in which Supercargo is stretched out on the bar with his hands across his chest like a dead man underscores his role as the scapegoat sacrificed for the sins of his people.

Invested with power by whites, who rely on him to keep the vets *under control*, Supercargo also represents the white power structure. Consequently, the vets, who are unable to directly attack their white oppressors, vent their pain and frustration on Supercargo, who is beaten (possibly to death) when they finally get their hands on him. (In Chapter 6, the vet is escorted by Crenshaw, a new attendant.) The similarities between Supercargo and Tatlock, the blindfolded boxing match winner, are striking. Both are large, physically imposing men, and both are tokens singled out by whites to keep blacks in their place. Their role is much like that of the black plantation overseer who was often hated more than the slaveholder and who—because of his extreme self-hatred—was often excessively cruel and brutal.

Theme

The mechanical man imagery, first introduced in Chapter 2 when Trueblood imagines himself as the man inside the clock, is also important. Rather than being depicted as human beings, individuals are referred to as robots and cogs in the machine. This theme is advanced through the brief conversation between the narrator and Norton when, in response to the narrator's question, "Will you need me this evening, sir?" Norton responds, "No, I won't be needing the machine."

Glossary

General Pershing   General John Joseph Pershing (1860–1948), a veteran of the Spanish-American War (1898) who was named by President Woodrow Wilson as commander of the American Expeditionary Forces in World War I.

armistice   a temporary stopping of warfare by mutual agreement, as a truce preliminary to the signing of a peace treaty. Armistice Day (November 11), now known as Veteran's Day, marks the anniversary of the armistice of World War I in 1918.

Tell him we don't jimcrow nobody   Jim Crow laws were designed to legalize discrimination against blacks.

Thomas Jefferson   American statesman (1743–1826), third president of the United States (1801–1809), drew up the Declaration of Independence. Recent revelations concerning the relationship between Thomas Jefferson and his black mistress, Sally Heming, focused renewed attention on America's system of chattel slavery.

fungo-hitter   a batter who hits a fly ball after he has himself tossed the baseball into the air.

balustrade   a railing held up by small posts, or balusters, as on a staircase.

homburg   a man's felt hat with a crown dented front to back and a stiffened brim turned up slightly at the sides.

moiling   marked by confusion and turmoil.

Chapters 5–6

Summary

Attending chapel, the narrator hears Rev. Homer A. Barbee, a blind preacher from Chicago, deliver a powerful sermon about the Founder and his vision for the college. Overcome with emotion, the narrator leaves early to prepare for his meeting with Dr. Bledsoe. During the meeting, he is shocked to discover that Bledsoe, entrusted with carrying on the Founder's legacy, is nothing like the man Rev. Barbee built him up to be. That evening, after Bledsoe reveals his greedy, self-serving, and opportunistic character to the narrator, lecturing him on the politics of race and power, Bledsoe expels the narrator. Devastated, the narrator decides to leave immediately, returning to Bledsoe's office only to pick up seven letters that, Bledsoe assures, will help him get a job in New York where he can earn enough money to return to school in the fall. Grateful for his assistance, the narrator accepts the letters and places them in his briefcase along with his high school diploma.

Commentary

These chapters reveal that, instead of preserving and protecting the Founder's legacy, Dr. Bledsoe perpetuates the myth of white supremacy by educating his students to stay in their *place*, subservient to whites. Thus, as the narrator suspects as he ponders the statue of the Founder lifting the veil, Bledsoe is, in fact, lowering the veil and ensuring that his students remain "in the dark."

Although they seem very different, Rev. Barbee and Dr. Bledsoe are similar in some ways. (See Character Analyses.) The most striking resemblance between the two men is that both are blind to the truth and therefore "in the dark" about the ways of the world. But while Rev. Barbee is physically blind and cannot see things as they are, Dr. Bledsoe is emotionally blind and simply refuses to see, which is far more debilitating.

Here again, Ellison skillfully merges fact and fiction. Bledsoe and Barbee allude to the two sides of a renowned historical figure: Booker T. Washington, the Founder of Alabama's Tuskegee Institute. Praised by some as a powerful leader and educator, Washington was condemned by others—such as the famous black scholar and educator W.E.B. Du Bois—for his conciliatory stance on "social equality." Although his intentions were good, Washington was blind to the impact his conciliatory stance had on blacks who were determined to fight for equal rights at any cost.

Bledsoe reveals, through his sermon, that he once idolized the Founder in the same way the narrator idolizes Bledsoe (until he discovers his true character). While Bledsoe (like the narrator) despises lower-class blacks, he cannot deny the racial and cultural ties that bind him to "these people." Like Trueblood, Bledsoe is a blues singer and storyteller. But unlike Trueblood—who remains true to his blood (people)—Bledsoe betrays his people. Rev. Barbee's sermon infers that Dr. Bledsoe was once an idealistic young man like the narrator who truly believed in the Founder's dream. But—as is revealed through Bledsoe's ensuing conversation with the narrator painful experiences as a black man in a racist white society so distorted his vision that he can no longer see the dream.

During his fateful meeting with Bledsoe, the narrator learns some valuable lessons concerning the politics of race and power. Bledsoe's rhetorical question, "What kind of education are you getting around here?" seems to confuse the narrator as he struggles to tell his side of the story concerning Norton's disastrous campus tour. In light of Rev. Barbee's powerful sermon concerning the Founder's dream of bringing black people out of the darkness and ignorance of slavery into the light of knowledge through education, Bledsoe's question seems particularly poignant, as it highlights the contrast between "the way things are and the way they're supposed to be."

Still haunted by the horrors of slavery, which legally denied blacks the right to read and write, blacks saw education as a means of obtaining a measure of pride and dignity and an opportunity for a better life. Along with men such as Booker T. Washington, the founder of Tuskegee Institute—which serves as the model for Ellison's nameless Southern college—blacks believed that education would provide a way out of the crushing cycle of poverty experienced by sharecroppers and tenant farmers, in addition to forcing whites to see them as intelligent, articulate human beings instead of brutes ideally suited for working in the fields and performing other types of hard, menial labor. Moreover, teaching people to become independent, critical thinkers and transmitting the culture and history of a people are two of education's primary goals. Neither goal, however, plays a part in Bledsoe's philosophy of education.

Literary Device

Key images in these two chapters include the surreal image of Rev. Barbee's collar cutting off his head, symbolizing the separation of mind and body (because blacks were not allowed to integrate their mind and body and become whole men), and the statue of the Founder soiled by the mockingbird, symbolizing the white stain on black history.

The role of religion, the power of *sermonic language* with its drama, biblical imagery, and emphatic repetition, and the impact of the black church on the black community, are also significant. Although Ellison focuses on the importance of the church, through Rev. Barbee's blindness he also wants to point out that blind faith without some grounding in reality is of little use to the black community. Returning to the images of the blindfolds and the veil, Ellison is alluding to the fact that religion was often used to keep blacks "in their place," as white preachers often preached sermons centering on the theme, "Slaves, be obedient to them that are your masters." He is also trying to point out that surviving in this world necessitates both a spiritual vision as well as a firm grasp on reality.

Bledsoe, playing the role of the college gatekeeper, jealously guards his position. Afraid that someone like the narrator—whom he sees as a potential threat—will undermine his authority and challenge the status quo, Bledsoe gets rid of him immediately.

Glossary

vespers   evening prayer.

verbena   any of various plants with spikes or clusters of showy red, white, or purplish flowers, widely grown for ornament.

arpeggios   chords played so that the notes of each chord are played in quick succession instead of simultaneously.

nexus   a connection, tie, or link between individuals of a group, members of a series, etc.

Horatio Alger   American author (1832–99). Alger sold more than 200 million books after the Civil War by writing about characters such as "Ragged Dick" and "Poorhouse Jed," who overcame incredible odds to succeed in life. His name has come to symbolize the journey from rags to riches.

dugs   a female animal's nipples, teats, etc.; sometimes used, vulgarly or contemptuously, in reference to a woman's breasts.

Aristotle   ancient Greek philosopher, pupil of Plato; noted for works on logic, metaphysics, ethics, politics, etc.

Mother Hubbards   full, loose gowns for women, patterned after the costume worn by Mother Hubbard, a character in a nursery rhyme.

alpacas   a thin cloth woven from the wool of a llama, often mixed with other fibers.

diminuendo   a gradual decrease in loudness.

Your arms are too short to box with me, son   reference to the black folk saying, "Your arms are too short to box with God."

Chapters 7–9

Summary

Leaving college on a bus headed for New York, the narrator meets the vet from the Golden Day, who is being transferred to St. Elizabeth's (a mental hospital in Washington, D.C.), and his new attendant, Crenshaw. The vet reminisces about his first trip north to Chicago and speculates about the exciting new things the narrator is bound to experience in New York. He also tells the narrator that he hoped for a transfer to Washington, D.C., for a long time but wonders what brought it about so suddenly. As the bus reaches its next stop and they go their separate ways, he gives the narrator some last-minute advice about surviving in New York.

Arriving in New York, the narrator takes the subway to Harlem, where he is amazed to see so many black people. He is especially surprised to see an angry black man with a West Indian accent addressing a group of black men in the street without being arrested. After passing the group, the narrator asks two white policemen for directions to Men's House, where he registers, immediately goes to his room, and takes out his packet of letters, planning his job search.

Over the next several days, the narrator distributes six of the letters from Dr. Bledsoe, only to meet with polite but firm refusals. Worried about his lack of a job, the narrator decides to change his tactics: He writes a letter to Mr. Emerson, requesting an appointment and explaining that he has a message from Dr. Bledsoe. He also writes a letter to Mr. Norton offering his services. After three days, he is disappointed by the complete lack of replies, but resolves to remain optimistic, even though his money is almost gone. The next morning, he feels confident that his luck has changed when he receives a letter from Mr. Emerson.

On his way to meet with Mr. Emerson, the narrator encounters an old man singing a familiar blues song and pushing a cart filled with discarded blueprints. Although the narrator is at first alarmed by the cartman, whose nonsensical riddles and rhymes remind him of the vet at the Golden Day, he gradually begins to relax and recognizes some of the rhymes as songs from his childhood. Next, the narrator stops at a drugstore for breakfast. Upset with the counterman's suggestion, "the special"—pork chops, grits, eggs, biscuits, and coffee—because the counterman has correctly identified him as being from the South, the narrator orders orange juice, toast, and coffee instead. As he leaves the drugstore, he seems surprised to see the counterman serving "the special" to a white man.

Finally arriving at Mr. Emerson's office, the narrator is met by a young man who identifies himself as Mr. Emerson's son, then reveals the devastating contents of Dr. Bledsoe's letter. Aware of the shock his revelation has on the narrator, young Mr. Emerson first offers him a job as his valet and then offers to get him a job at Liberty Paints, but the narrator refuses both offers.

Back in his room, he experiences the full impact of Bledsoe's betrayal. Emboldened by rage, he calls Liberty Paints and is surprised to be offered an interview. That night, his dreams of revenge make it hard for him to sleep.

Commentary

These three chapters mark a major transition in the narrator's life as he leaves his beloved college behind and heads north to New York. Traveling from the South to the North (South Carolina to New York), the narrator traces the path of millions of blacks who left the South in droves to seek a new life in the North during the Great Migration (1930–45), headed for cities like Chicago, Detroit, and New York. But unlike these individuals who left the South with a sense of hope and promise, relieved to leave behind the back-breaking labor of the plantation life, the narrator doesn't want to leave his beloved college. In fact, the only thing that sustains him is the thought of returning to the campus as soon as he earns enough money to continue his education and gained Dr. Bledsoe's forgiveness.

Theme

The narrator's conversation with the vet on the bus illustrates his continuing blindness to events around him. While the vet reminisces about his own adventures in Chicago and talks about all the exciting things the narrator has to look forward to, the narrator never stops to ask the vet why he returned to the South, nor does he make any conscious connections between the vet's transfer to Washington, D.C., and his own "transfer" to New York. Instead, he worries that the vet may become violent and resents being forced to sit with him and Crenshaw in the Jim Crow section of the bus.

At this point, the narrator has not yet recognized the power of words as weapons and draws no connection between the vet's violent outburst at the Golden Day and his own violent outburst in Dr. Bledsoe's office. Nor does he recall the violent impact of his grandfather's dying words or the battle royal. Only when he discovers the contents of Dr. Bledsoe's letters does he become fully aware of the formidable power wielded by those who use words as weapons.

Literary Device

The narrator's first dream-like impressions of New York differ radically from Richard Wright's first impressions of Chicago in *Black Boy*, in which he describes the city as "unreal." The shock of being transported from the agrarian South to the industrial North seems to demand tremendous adjustment and adaptation from blacks who found themselves suddenly uprooted from their homes and thrust into an alien culture where the laws of the South no longer apply. (At this point, the narrator has not yet discovered that even though he has infinitely more freedom than he had in the South, the Northern version of covert racism is just as devastating as the overt racism of the South.)

Finally safe in his room at Men's House, the narrator concludes that Harlem is an unreal city of dreams where none of the old rules seem to apply. His first instinct is to fall back on religion (symbolized by the Gideon Bible on his nightstand), but he rejects that notion, deciding that because it reminds him of home, it will only make him homesick. Next, he considers reading the letters, but reasons that by doing so, he would be violating Dr. Bledsoe's trust. In short, the narrator struggles to hold on to his values, but soon discovers that the rules of right and wrong don't always apply in a world where people arbitrarily change the rules to suit the circumstances. In this way, Ellison advances the theme of game-playing, which is emphasized by the narrator's comparing the letters to "a hand of high trump cards."

Through the narrator's encounter with the counterman at the diner and the blues-singing cart-man with his discarded blueprints (who identifies himself as Peter Wheatstraw), the chapters also explore the role of black culture through folklore and food. [Peetie (or Pete) Wheatstraw was the stage name of William Bunch, a blues singer who produced more than 160 recording between 1930 and 1941. The name was also a pseudonym adopted by other singers.]

From his encounter with the cart-man, the narrator learns that he cannot escape his past, or his Southern "roots." He also learns that in order to live in New York, he must learn not only to survive, but to adapt. Providing a sharp contrast to the cart-man, Mr. Emerson's son admits to feeling somewhat guilty, yet openly revels in his father's material wealth, leading the narrator to conclude that "these men must be kings of the earth." Like Mr. Norton, Mr. Emerson has exploited blacks for his personal gain, as illustrated by the opulent artwork and furnishings of his office, which the narrator refers to as "a museum." But unlike the museum at his college, which housed only the relics of slavery, Mr. Emerson's "museum" includes priceless treasures from Asia and Africa, symbolizing the exploitation of both continents by Europeans. Suggesting imminent danger and recalling animalistic behaviors in both the battle royal and Golden Day episodes, the jungle imagery is also significant.

The relationship between Mr. Emerson and his son who, appears to be homosexual, is important as well. Having experienced the pain of rejection and alienation himself, Mr. Emerson's son can identify with the narrator, which prompts him to reveal the contents of Dr. Bledsoe's letter. The narrator describes young Emerson as "moving with a long, hip-swinging stride," a phrase used earlier to describe the vet, thereby drawing our attention to the similarities between blacks and whites while simultaneously highlighting the vast differences in their social and economic status. When the narrator returns to his room at Men's House and acknowledges the full impact of Dr. Bledsoe's betrayal, he initially feels that his life is over and sets his sights on revenge. But his rage prompts him to call Liberty Paints for, as he points out, "I had to have a job and I took what I hoped was the quickest means." Ultimately, the narrator is driven by his need for economic survival, which, as in subsequent chapters, provides the catalyst for many of his rash and impulsive actions.

Glossary

allow me to chew the rag   slang for "let me speak freely" or "indulge me."

Red Cap   a baggage porter as in a railroad station, easily identified by his red cap.

the belly of a frantic whale   Biblical allusion to the story of Jonah and the Whale. Jonah is often represented as the bearer of bad luck.

staccato   made up of abrupt, distinct elements or sounds.

Huckleberry   reference to Mark Twain's classic novel, *Huckleberry Finn*, the story of Huckleberry Finn, a Southern white boy, and his friendship with the runaway slave, "Nigger Jim."

Charlie Chaplin pants   Charlie Chaplin (Sir Charles Spencer Chaplin, 1889–1977), an English film actor, director, and producer, was a famous comedian in the United States, noted for wearing big, oversized pants and playing a loveable clown in films such as *The Little Tramp*.

Totem and Taboo   a book by Austrian physician and neurologist Sigmund Freud (1856–1939), hailed as the founder of psycho-analysis. Published in 1913, *Totem and Taboo* elaborates on Freud's theories of the division of the unconscious mind into the *id*, the *ego*, and the *super-ego*.

aviary   a large cage or building for keeping many birds.

helical   having the form of a helix or spiral.

rookery   a colony of rooks (European crows) or swindlers (cheats).

Chapters 10–12

Summary

Arriving at Liberty Paints, the narrator is greeted by a large electric sign that reads "Keep America Pure with Liberty Paints." After a brief interview with the personnel manager, he is assigned to work for a Mr. Kimbro, referred to by his employees as "the colonel" and "slave driver." As an office boy escorts him to Kimbro's office, located in a building with a pure white hall, the narrator learns that the factory makes paint for the government and that he is one of six "colored college boys" hired to replace union workers out on strike.

This ominous overview of the narrator's work environment fore-shadows the disastrous events of the rest of his day, which turns into a virtual nightmare as the narrator has conflicts with both Kimbro and his second supervisor, Lucius Brockway, a black man who maintains the factory's boilers in the basement. A long-time employee of Liberty Paints, Brockway helped create the company's slogan, "If It's Optic White, It's the Right White." The narrator's confrontation with Brockway escalates into a physical fight, during which the narrator knocks out the old man's false teeth. To retaliate, Brockway rigs the boilers to explode, sending the narrator to the factory hospital.

At the hospital, the narrator is subjected to a painful series of electric shocks, which leave him feeling strangely disconnected from his body and unable to express his anger and indignation. Finally, the doctors release him, declare him "cured," and take him three floors down to see the hospital director. The director tells the narrator that he is not "prepared for work under . . . industrial conditions," asks him to sign a release form absolving the company of any responsibility for his injuries, and assures him that he will be compensated later.

Disoriented and confused, the narrator finds his way back to the subway and returns to Harlem, where he is taken in by a kindly black woman named Mary Rambo, who nurtures him back to health.

Commentary

Although the Liberty Paint Factory and factory hospital episodes may seem bizarre, they make sense from a historical perspective.

Style & Language

Ellison's depiction of the Liberty Paint Factory challenges some of our most cherished symbols of freedom, illustrating, once again, that the reality of black Americans in the United States is quite different from that of white Americans. One such symbol is the Statue of Liberty, which welcomes immigrants to America, promising freedom, equality, and justice. But arriving from Harlem, the narrator is met not by the Statue of Liberty, but by a paint factory with a similar name that manufactures optic white paint, thus turning America's metaphorical melting pot into a paint bucket. In like manner, Ellison turns the American bald eagle into the screaming eagle that serves as the logo for the paint factory with its *white-is-right* philosophy. The white paint symbolizes America's refusal to accept the diversity of its citizens and its attempt to whitewash or cover up the issue of racism.

Character Insight

Brockway is the proverbial *old dog* who refuses to learn new tricks. Having been with the company since its inception, he refuses to acknowledge that times have changed. Instead of welcoming the narrator and treating him as a possible protégé, he resents his presence, feeling threatened by him. And, suspecting the narrator attended a secret union meeting, Brockway attacks him—first verbally, then physically—without giving him a chance to explain what happened. Although angry at his false accusations, the narrator decides that Brockway is just a harmless old dog whose bark is worse than his bite (as indicated by Brockway's losing his false teeth). Unfortunately, the narrator learns—too late—that he underestimated the old man, who gets his revenge by rigging the explosion.

In many ways, the narrator's confrontation with Brockway echoes his final confrontation with Dr. Bledsoe, who also refuses to listen to him. Bledsoe and Brockway share numerous common characteristics: Both are gatekeepers, fiercely protective of their domain; both use their power to promote their own selfish interests; and both rely on past connections with powerful white men to safeguard their positions. As Brockway tells the narrator how he first got his job, his relationship to Old Man Sparland, the founder of Liberty Paints, becomes apparent, bearing similarity to Bledsoe's relationship to the Founder.

The factory hospital episode in Chapter 11 advances the theme of dual realities for blacks and whites. Before the passage of the Civil Rights Act of 1965, all public facilities in the U.S. were segregated, which meant that blacks could not receive medical care in white hospitals. The narrator's sense of fear and panic at finding himself at the factory hospital following the explosion at Liberty Paints is conceivable. Unlike white patients, who would expect to find kind, sympathetic doctors and nurses prepared to tend to their wounds and relieve their pain, black patients would understandably feel vulnerable at the thought of being at the mercy of white doctors and nurses.

As an educated black man, the narrator is not oblivious to the animosity of the white medical establishment toward blacks. He is undoubtedly aware of cases such as that of world-renowned surgeon, scientist, and educator Charles Richard Drew (1904–50). The pioneer of blood plasma preservation, Dr. Drew established the first successful blood plasma bank. In 1950, while on his way to a medical convention at Tuskegee Institute, Dr. Drew was fatally injured in a car accident. Denied treatment at a nearby white hospital, he was refused the blood transfusion that might have saved his life.

The narrator's horrific experience in the factory hospital alludes to the experiences of blacks subjected to the infamous Tuskegee Study (1932–72), in which a group of poor black men were used as guinea pigs by the U.S. Government to determine the effects of untreated syphilis on the human body. In 1973, after settling a class-action lawsuit, the government distributed approximately $10 million to more than 6,000 survivors and their families. In 1999, President Clinton publicly apologized to four survivors of the study, which historians have described as "one of the most shameful episodes in American history."

The events in Chapter 11 mirror the events in Chapter 1, as the narrator undergoes a second rite of passage. But whereas the battle royal represented the narrator's initiation into a chaotic world of violence and brutality, the factory hospital episode represents his rebirth into a new reality.

Literary Device

Like Chapter 1, Chapter 11 was also published independently as a short story, "Out of the Hospital and Under the Bar" (presumably because the narrator discovers that the hospital is built on top of a tavern). The story was part of the original manuscript of *Invisible Man*, but the text was drastically altered by Ellison's editor. In both Chapter 11 and the short story, Ellison draws some profound parallels between the hospital and the bar. Like the Golden Day in Chapter 3, the factory hospital has undergone numerous transformations. In the social hierarchy of black America, the bar, which serves as a refuge and sanctuary from the white world, is more important than the hospital, which is simply an extension of the violent and racist white world. The Golden Day plays a vital part in helping the vets maintain their sanity, a function that is not provided by the mental health profession.

During his confinement to the hospital, the narrator, like the vets, is cast into the role of *inmate* (vs. *patient*). Birth imagery interspersed with frequent references to tools and instruments underscores the image of man as machine and the narrator as a macabre creation of Dr. Frankenstein. For instance, the narrator (who has been repeatedly entranced by music and musical instruments) now envisions himself as an instrument (an accordion) being played by two men who are not musicians, but doctors.

The narrator's move from Men's House to Mary's house marks a major transition in his life. Having lived through the factory hospital nightmare, the narrator has been forced to surrender his illusions. He can no longer relate to the men at Men's House who, like the vets at the Golden Day, still cling desperately to their illusions, which enable them to ignore the brutal realities of their daily lives. (Men's House is modeled after the Harlem branch of New York's YMCA, where Ellison spent several months following his move to New York.)

Glossary

play the dozens a form of verbal play in which the participants exchange witty, ribald taunts and insults, often specifically about each other's mother; used first, and chiefly, by African Americans.

Lenox Avenue The intersection of Lenox Avenue and 135th Street marks the heart of Harlem.

ofay slang term for "white person." One critic conjectures that "ofay" is pig Latin for "foe."

Chapter 13

Summary

The next day, while walking in the streets of Harlem, the narrator buys a hot buttered yam from a street vendor and eats it greedily. No longer feeling compelled to hide his identity as a Southern black by denying his love for certain foods, the narrator experiences a profound sense of freedom. Pondering the link between food and identity, he imagines exposing Dr. Bledsoe as "a shameless chitterling eater," then runs back to the vendor and buys two more yams, but discovers that the last one is frostbitten.

Continuing on, the narrator comes upon the scene of an eviction. Two white men bring a chest of drawers out of a nearby apartment while a group of black men and women stand silently by and an old black woman tearfully calls the narrator's attention to her helplessness and humiliation. Feeling uncomfortable, the narrator tries to blend into the crowd of bystanders. Oblivious to the pleas of her husband, who has appeared on the scene to comfort her, the woman loudly denounces the men who are literally tearing her home apart.

The narrator surveys their meager belongings, which represent a whole lifetime of struggle. Suddenly overwhelmed with emotion, he realizes that an old, yellowed piece of paper that has been trampled into the snow is the old man's "freedom papers." The narrator picks up the precious document and places it in the chest of drawers.

As the woman tries to go back into her house to pray, one of the white men tries to stop her and a scuffle ensues, during which the old woman falls and angry bystanders surge forward. Determined to stop the tension from erupting into violence, the narrator intercedes and pleads for the men to remain calm and to consider the consequences of their actions. Launching an emotional speech on dispossession, the narrator encourages them to return all the furnishings to the apartment and leads them into the old couple's house to pray.

Meanwhile, the police arrive and accuse the narrator of interfering with the eviction, but a white girl helps him escape by suggesting that he run across the apartment rooftops. After narrowly escaping the police, the narrator encounters a man who introduces himself as Brother Jack. After telling the narrator how much he admired his speech at the eviction, Brother Jack invites the narrator to accompany him to a nearby diner. There, Brother Jack invites the narrator to join the Brotherhood. Skeptical, the narrator refuses and heads back to Mary's, but he accepts a slip of paper containing Brother Jack's name and address.

Commentary

**Style &
Language**

The narrator's determination to *continue on the yam level* by embracing rather than rejecting his black culture is one of the highlights of this chapter. His quip, "I yam what I yam," which initially appears to be simply another example of Ellison's wordplay, is, on closer analysis, much more complex. The phrase is from *Popeye*, the cartoon character who is part of our American pop culture, just as yams are part of the narrator's Southern culture. Considering his comment from this perspective, eating yams in public indicates his having overcome his shame at being identified as a Southern Negro, which marks an important turning point in his quest for identity. (Recall, for example, his refusal to order the *special* of pork chops, grits, eggs, hot biscuits, and coffee in Chapter 9.)

The phrase also alludes to French mathematician and philosopher Rene Descartes' famous statement, "I think; therefore, I am," which highlights rational thought as the definitive attribute of the individual. Ironically, it also foreshadows the 1960s Civil Rights movement during which black men marched in silent protest, carrying signs and wearing sandwich boards proclaiming, "I am a man!"

The fact that the narrator arrives at this defining moment shortly after he revels in his vision of exposing Dr. Bledsoe as a "chitterling eater" is significant because he suddenly realizes that his black Southern culture (symbolized by traditional Southern foods such as yams and chitterlings) is part of his identity. However, although he has gone from one extreme to the other—first denying, then embracing his cultural heritage—he has not come any closer to establishing his personal identity.

The conversation between the narrator and Brother Jack concerning the eviction of Brother and Sister Provo is another important aspect of this chapter. Seeing that the narrator has been emotionally touched by the scene, Brother Jack pretends to empathize with him by comparing the eviction to "a death" and then telling him about *Death on the City Pavements*, which he describes as "a detective story or something I read somewhere. . . ." In fact, "Death on the City Pavements" is not a detective story, but an allusion to Part 3 of Richard Wright's *12 Million Black Voices*, a pictorial history of black America. Published in 1941, the book combines Wright's text with photographs compiled during the Great Depression, which illustrate the crushing poverty of rural blacks living in squalid shacks in the South and urban blacks living in northern ghettos. "Death on the City Pavements" focuses on the hopelessness and despair of Harlem residents living in crowded, substandard, and overpriced apartments. In light of Wright's graphic essay, the evictions of blacks in Harlem, such as that witnessed by the narrator, were common, everyday events. But Brother Jack's lack of knowledge concerning "Death on the City Pavements" reveals his lack of knowledge concerning African American culture and literature and, by extension, his lack of knowledge about the plight of Harlem's black citizens, whom his organization purports to support and represent.

The women in the eviction scene are also significant. The men are spurred into action by an unidentified West Indian woman, and Sister Provo defies the white men attempting to evict her and her husband. Their actions illustrate the powerful although largely unacknowledged role of black women in the struggle for freedom and equality.

Character Insight

It seems that witnessing the eviction profoundly alters the narrator's perception of Harlem and raises his awareness of his social responsibility to the black community. On his arrival, he saw Harlem as a city of dreams, where black girls work at a five-and-dime store and black policemen direct traffic. After the eviction, he sees Harlem as just another dismal, impoverished black neighborhood.

Glossary

Nubian   a native or inhabitant of Nubia, an ancient kingdom in Northeast Africa.

honey wagon   slang for a wagon used to transport human body waste. Honey wagons were used before the advent of indoor toilets.

paddie   slang version of *paddyroller,* a slave catcher who hunted runaways for bounty.

fyce   a small, snappish dog.

Chapters 14–16

Summary

Returning to Mary's, the narrator is overwhelmed by the odor of cabbage, which reminds him of his impoverished childhood. The odor also makes him realize that cabbage is probably all Mary can afford, because he is still behind in his rent. Later, as he lies in bed listening to Mary singing, he resolves to be more responsible and decides to call Brother Jack to discuss his job offer.

The narrator is surprised to find that Brother Jack apparently expected his call, because he immediately gives the narrator directions to an address on Lenox Avenue. When the narrator arrives at the designated address, a car pulls up to the curb with three men inside, plus Brother Jack, who tells him to get in and informs him that they are going to a party. After a short ride through Central Park, the car stops and the men enter the Chthonian, an exclusive private club, where they are met by a sophisticated woman (later identified as Emma). Wondering about the contrast between the room's lavish decor and the men's poor clothing, the narrator surveys the scene. Brother Jack guides him into a larger, even more lavishly decorated room filled with well-dressed people. The narrator overhears Emma asking Jack if he thinks that the narrator is black enough to be an effective leader. Deeply offended by her remark, the narrator crosses to a nearby window where he remains lost in thought. Soon the narrator is asked to join a group in the library where he is given a new name and informed that he will be the new Booker T. Washington.

In the midst of the celebration, a belligerent drunk demands that the narrator sing an old Negro spiritual. Before the narrator can respond, Brother Jack orders the forcible removal of the man from the room, and the crowd lapses into an embarrassed silence, finally broken by the narrator's near-hysterical laughter. After numerous apologies Emma asks the narrator to dance, and the party resumes.

Later that night, back at Mary's, the narrator decides that it would be best to simply place his rent money on the table the following morning, in order to avoid an emotional farewell scene with Mary, and move into the apartment Brother Jack provided for him.

The next morning, he is awakened by the sounds of someone banging on the steam pipes. He looks for something to use to strike the pipes and discovers Mary's coin-filled, cast-iron bank in the shape of "a very black, red-lipped, and wide-mouthed Negro," which he finds obscene and repulsive. He bangs on the pipes with the bank, it shatters, and he frantically tries to hide the broken pieces and gather up the coins. But when Mary knocks on the door and tells him to come to the kitchen for breakfast, he hastily stuffs the pieces into his coat pocket, planning to get rid of them on the way downtown.

Realizing that he has no choice but to speak to Mary, he goes into the kitchen and tries to give her a hundred-dollar bill, which she at first refuses to accept. Suddenly, the kitchen is invaded by a horde of roaches that have been shaken loose from the steam pipes. After helping Mary kill the roaches and clean up the kitchen, he leaves to go shopping for his new clothes and to find his new apartment. Along the way, he tries unsuccessfully to get rid of the broken bank, but finally decides to add it to the items in his briefcase.

Later that evening, Brother Jack picks him up and takes him to an old sports arena in Harlem, the site of the Brotherhood rally where he is to give his first speech. Across the dressing room, tacked to a wall, a faded photograph of a former boxing champion blinded in the ring reminds the narrator of the stories his grandfather told him about the boxer. Finally called to the podium, the narrator delivers a passionate speech on dispossession, and is bewildered when Brother Jack and several other members of the Brotherhood criticize his speech for being "incorrect." The evening ends with Brother Jack informing the narrator to report to Brother Hambro for training in scientific rhetoric.

Back in his apartment, the narrator reflects on his speech and realizes that he spoke spontaneously and from the heart. Pondering over exactly what he meant by declaring that by joining the Brotherhood, he felt "more human," he recalls a lecture from his former literature teacher, Mr. Woodridge, on the problem of Stephen Daedalus. He also reflects on how his rejection and betrayal by Dr. Bledsoe and Mr. Norton brought him to the Brotherhood. As he drifts off to sleep, he imagines the leadership potential available to him through the Brotherhood and resolves to take full advantage of his new position.

Commentary

These three chapters, which focus on the narrator's induction into the Brotherhood, analyze his transformation from an independent individual to a member of a powerful political organization that promises to make him a community leader, but treats him like a puppet. The narrator's naïve willingness to accept Brother Jack's orders without question is striking. Eager to be a leader, the narrator meekly accepts his new name, his new apartment, and his proposed role as the new Booker T. Washington.

Chapters 14 through 16 also trace the narrator's transformation as he moves from the warmth and safety of Mary's house to the coldness and danger of the Brotherhood. The numerous references to surprise underscore the uncertainty and danger that await the narrator as he plunges into the underworld of the Brotherhood. This uncertainty is characterized by his initial visit to the Chthonian, where nothing is what it appears to be, beginning with the door knocker that turns out to be a door bell. The scene in which the narrator attempts to give Mary the hundred-dollar bill is also important because it recalls the scene in Chapter 2 in which the narrator resents the fact that Mr. Norton gives Jim Trueblood a hundred-dollar bill.

Shopping for new clothes and attempting to rid himself of Mary's cast-iron bank, the narrator does his best to rid himself of his old identity in preparation for his induction into the Brotherhood. Lacking a positive self-image, the narrator sees Mary's bank as a grossly distorted caricature of himself. (Note the narrator's remark that his head feels as if it is about to explode. Minutes later, as he bangs the bank against the pipes, the bank's head *explodes*.) Viewed from another perspective, the bank also represents the racist symbols and images that still pervade our culture, perpetuating the destructive *Sambo* stereotype.

The scene in which the narrator tries desperately to rid himself of his "shattered image" offers a unique twist on the themes of invisibility and identity. Normally, a black man walking down the streets of Harlem early in the morning would be virtually invisible, yet this particular morning, the narrator is highly visible. While he is simply trying to throw away some trash, his actions are perceived as being much more significant by two bystanders who interpret what he does based on their perception of who he is. The Northern mulatto woman sees him as a Southern "field nigger," with no respect for personal property, the Southern man sees him as a slick New York Negro/con artist. Even though both share his racial identity, neither identifies with him on the basis of race, choosing instead to see him as an outsider on the basis of regional, cultural, and class differences, thus shattering the image of the homogeneous, one-dimensional black community.

The narrator's arrival at the Chthonian marks a dramatic change in his environment, as he moves from the warmth and safety of Mary's house into a cold, white world of danger and violence. The narrator also moves from a world of sound (symbolized by Mary's singing) to a world of silence (symbolized by the musical instruments suspended by the neck and the silent radio at the Chthonian).

Style & Language

As in previous chapters, these chapters provide numerous examples of Ellison's wordplay. For example, when the narrator hesitates about joining the Brotherhood, Brother Jack remarks, "It's a party; you might like it." *Party* can refer to either a social event or a political group.

Glossary

dunning   demanding payment of a debt.

"Back Water Blues"   song made famous by blues singer Bessie Smith (1894–1937), known as "The Empress of the Blues."

Chthonian   of the underworld of the dead and its gods or spirits.

Sun Yat-sen   Chinese political and revolutionary leader (1866–1925).

Danny O'Connell   Irish nationalist leader (1775–1847).

tam   short for tam-o'-shanter, a Scottish cap with a wide, round, flat top and, often, a center pompom.

pince-nez   eyeglass without temples, kept in place by a spring gripping the bridge of the nose.

Nijinskys   referring to the dancer's artistic movements; pluralized proper name of Vaslav Nijinsky (1890–1950), famous male Russian ballet dancer known for his leaps and jumps.

dialectics   the art of logical argumentation.

James Joyce, William Yeats, and Sean O'Casey   Irish authors whose works focused on the lives of the working class.

Stephen's problem   allusion to Stephen Dedalus, the protagonist of James Joyce's autobiographical novel, *Portrait of the Artist as a Young Man*. In the novel, Stephen represents the individual struggling against society to realize himself as an artist. Stephen believes his name provides a spiritual link to Daedalus, the mythological Greek inventor who created the Labyrinth for King Minos of Crete, in which he and his son Icarus eventually found themselves imprisoned.

Chapter 17

Summary

After learning the art of scientific rhetoric for four months, the narrator receives an invitation over the phone to go for a ride from Brother Jack. Expecting to go to the Chthonian, the narrator is disappointed when Brother Jack takes him to the El Toro Bar instead. But the narrator is excited to hear Brother Jack tell him that he has been appointed chief spokesman of the Brotherhood's Harlem District. Brother Jack takes the narrator to visit his new office, and introduces him to Brother Tarp, an elderly black man who seems genuinely glad to meet the narrator.

The next morning at a Brotherhood meeting, the narrator is introduced to the other members of the Brotherhood as the new spokesman. Meeting Brother Tod Clifton, Harlem's youth director, the narrator senses that he might be a competitor for his new leadership position. Later, realizing that Brother Clifton is not interested in power or politics, he begins to relax and the two young men discuss their strategies for working with the Harlem community.

Leaving the Brotherhood meeting, Brother Clifton and the narrator are attacked by a group of black men led by Ras the Exhorter. The narrator sees Ras strike Brother Clifton and raise his knife threateningly, then lower it and walk away. As the narrator and Brother Clifton start to leave, Ras accuses Brother Clifton of being a traitor. Furious at this accusation, Brother Clifton turns on Ras and knocks him out. Brother Clifton and the narrator walk away, determined to ignore Ras and rededicate themselves to the Brotherhood.

Commentary

The events in this chapter create a growing sense of danger and foreboding, prompting the reader to feel that things are out of place and contrary to expectations.

To begin with, Brother Jack calls the narrator at midnight (the witching hour) and takes him not to the Chthonian, but to the El Toro

(Spanish for "The Bull"), a Harlem bar that caters not to blacks, but to a Spanish-speaking clientele. At the El Toro, as the narrator studies the scenes of a bullfight on the wall panels behind the bar, he notices a calendar with a picture of a white girl in a beer ad, indicating the date as April 1 (April Fool's Day). At this point, the narrator is indeed being *taken for a ride* or, to put it another way, he is being played for a fool and fed a lot of bull.

Another example of things being unexpected and out of place are the wall panels behind the bar. Expected to hold a mirror, they display bullfight scenes and a gored matador. Instead of seeing his own reflection, the narrator sees the matador's image—foreshadowing his own fate.

Theme

The scene also raises several issues that the narrator might question, especially after spending four months studying logic and scientific rhetoric. Why doesn't Brother Jack congratulate him on his new position, or announce his new position to the other Brotherhood members? What kind of a spokesman will he be if he will be told what he can and cannot say? Why, if he is to speak for the people of Harlem, did Brother Jack move him to an apartment outside his district? Most of all, he might consider the irony of having a white man assign him to be a spokesman for black people. But once again, the narrator fails to ask questions that might help him make sense of this situation.

The encounter that the narrator and Brother Clifton have with Ras and his men places their position in a new perspective, for while both men see themselves as leaders of the black community, Ras and his men see them as sellouts and *Uncle Toms*. Although Ras' ravings seem illogical and even racist, he does raise some significant issues, especially concerning the concept of *selling out*. In the black community, a *sellout* is a black person who accepts money or other personal gain by working for *the system* (the white power structure). This chapter raises the question: Is the narrator a sellout, or is he simply accepting a job that will enable him to earn a living by using his public speaking skills? A convincing case could probably be made for either side.

Although Ras's argument appears to be purely emotional, he makes several valid points concerning the tactics whites use to manipulate blacks. However, by focusing purely on race, his speech loses power. His remark that "all brothers are the same color" doesn't ring true. So far, the narrator suffered his most bitter betrayals at the hands of his black brothers such as Lucius Brockway and Dr. Bledsoe.

Representing socialism and Black Nationalism, respectively, Brother Jack and Ras characterize the contrast between the Brotherhood and Ras's followers. The Brotherhood supposedly advocates nonviolence and focuses on integration and cooperation as the only means by which people—both black and white—will be able to work together for the good of society as a whole, especially the poor and oppressed. In contrast, Ras's followers advocate freedom and equality even if it means fighting for these rights. The Brotherhood focuses on issues of both race and class, whereas Ras's followers emphasize race as the deciding factor.

Although Ellison insisted in a later essay that the Brotherhood does not represent Communism, the striking resemblance between the communist philosophy and the Brotherhood can't be ignored. Both emphasize group vs. individual rights. By contrast, Ras's Black Nationalist philosophy, although rooted in racism and separatism, stresses independence, self-reliance, and individual rights.

The Brotherhood may also represent the National Association for the Advancement of Colored People (NAACP) because it has been fraught with the same kinds of internal conflicts. Ellison undoubtedly knew that W.E.B. Du Bois, one of the NAACP's founders, eventually left the group because he felt it no longer fulfilled its mission as an active civil rights organization dedicated to fighting for equality and equal opportunity.

Another important development in Chapter 17 concerns the relationship between the narrator and Brother Clifton. Although Tod Clifton is *the darker brother*, he has distinctly European features. He also has already attained a leadership role within the Brotherhood. Conversely, the narrator, whom Emma describes as "not black enough" to represent the black community, is less steeped in Brotherhood philosophy and even admits that he has some doubts and misgivings about the organization. But like Brother Clifton, he sees the Brotherhood as a supportive organization that will help him hone his leadership skills and achieve his goal of becoming a renowned and respected speaker. On a more practical level, he also sees his work with the Brotherhood as a means of economic survival and an opportunity for a new life, as symbolized by his new clothes, new job, and new apartment, all of which he owes to the Brotherhood.

However, because both men are keenly aware that they have had to sacrifice many of their personal and cultural values to work for the Brotherhood, their encounter with Ras—who reminds them of their identity and responsibility to their African ancestors and the black community—is unsettling, especially for Brother Clifton.

Another key character introduced in this chapter is Brother Tarp, who gives the narrator a portrait of Frederick Douglass, indicating his faith in the narrator, whom he sees as having the potential to become another Douglass. A former slave, Douglass (1817–95) went on to become one of the most famous nineteenth-century orators and statesmen. By giving the narrator a portrait of Douglass for his office, Brother Tarp demonstrates his faith in him as a potential leader of the black community. His act also indicates that he views the narrator not as another Booker T. Washington, who many blacks felt compromised his values to gain the financial and political support of influential whites, but as another Douglass, a man who freed himself from the mental and physical bonds of slavery to become a renowned and respected spokesman for freedom and equality.

The narrator's initiation/indoctrination into the Brotherhood illustrates the process educated blacks (like Dr. Bledsoe) go through to be accepted into *the system*. Those who resist and refuse to play the game are often forced to the margins of society—such as Jim Trueblood, Mary, and the cart-man—or they are perceived as insane—such as the vet, the narrator's grandfather, and Ras the Exhorter. The narrator is, in fact, becoming Dr. Bledsoe, because the Brotherhood wants to make him the new Booker T. Washington.

Glossary

sectarianism   narrow-minded, limited, parochial thinking.

Uncle Tom   a term of contempt for a black whose behavior toward whites is regarded as fawning or servile.

perfidity   betrayal of trust; treachery.

Chapters 18–19

Summary

Opening his morning mail in his Harlem District office, the narrator discovers an unsigned letter, warning him not to "go too fast" and that "this is a white man's world." Distraught, he turns to Brother Tarp, who says not to worry about the letter, reassuring the narrator that he has lots of support. Brother Tarp tells the narrator about his imprisonment for more than 19 years because he dared to say "No" to a white man, and he gives the narrator a link from the chain he was forced to wear as an inmate. Although he doesn't know what to make of Brother Tarp's gift, the narrator is honored by his gesture.

Brother Wrestrum soon enters and, noticing the link of chain on the narrator's desk, recommends that he remove it, so as not to dramatize the racial differences between the black and white members of the Brotherhood. When the narrator objects to his remark, Brother Wrestrum cautions him that there are people in the Brotherhood who are only interested in using the organization for their own gain. Realizing that he has the narrator's attention, Brother Wrestrum informs him that Brother Tod Clifton struck a white man, not realizing that he was part of the Brotherhood. He points out that wearing Brotherhood emblems could prevent such incidents.

The narrator receives a call from a magazine, requesting an interview. Partly to spite Brother Wrestrum, he agrees to give the interview. About two weeks later, the narrator is shocked to learn that Brother Wrestrum has filed charges against him, accusing him of being an opportunist. The disciplinary committee revokes the narrator's leadership role as spokesman for the Harlem District and puts him in charge of *the Woman Question*. Angry and humiliated, the narrator leaves Harlem without saying goodbye to anyone.

At his first speaking engagement, the narrator is seduced by a white woman who pretends to be intrigued by his speech, but is actually attracted to his "primitive" qualities. When the woman's husband walks in on them, the narrator is horrified that the man does not seem to care.

The following day, at a meeting of the Brotherhood, the narrator learns that Brother Tod Clifton is missing.

Commentary

The anonymous letter left on the narrator's desk is yet another in a series of notes and letters that have a critical impact on the narrator's fate. Like Dr. Bledsoe's seven letters and the letter the narrator discovers in his briefcase in Chapter 1, the anonymous letter has a similar impact: It keeps him running. The anonymous letter warning him not to "go too fast" is essentially the same as the school superintendent's verbal warning in Chapter 1: "We mean to do right by you, but you've got to know your place at all times." The message also recapitulates Trueblood's comment, "I had to move without movin." The narrator is expected to project an image of progress (to support the image of the Brotherhood as a progressive, liberal organization without actually moving forward).

Literary Device

Brother Tarp's link of chain, symbolizing his escape from prison as well as his escape from mental slavery, contrasts with the smooth, unbroken chain on Dr. Bledsoe's desk. While Brother Tarp's chain represents his freedom, Dr. Bledsoe's chain is a reminder of his continued enslavement to power and materialism. Brother Wrestrum's obvious discomfort with the chain on the narrator's desk, a painful reminder of slavery, indicates that he is not comfortable with his racial and cultural identity.

Brother Wrestrum's low self-esteem and his desperate need to be recognized and respected are also reflected in his conversation with the narrator, revealing him to be precisely the type of opportunist he accuses the narrator of being. His suggestion that all Brotherhood members wear an emblem or insignia to identify each other provides the perfect opportunity for him to tell the narrator about Brother Tod Clifton's hitting a white man. Obviously aware of the potential power play between Brother Clifton and the narrator, he could be trying to ingratiate himself with the narrator, whom he perceives as being the man with the most power, by casting suspicion on Brother Clifton. When his plan fails and the narrator virtually ignores him, Brother Wrestrum decides to get even by openly challenging his leadership and authority.

The narrator's new position as spokesman on *the Woman Question* is also significant and somewhat humorous, considering the narrator's obvious lack of knowledge concerning women's issues. Although the details of his job are not revealed, his new platform presumably will focus on women's rights issues such as economic equity in the workplace. Because he himself has not achieved this equity, this situation is filled with irony. Once more, the Brotherhood's focus is on groups rather than on individuals, because their interest lies in addressing broad issues such as *the Woman Question* and the Negro problem rather than in helping individual women or Negroes.

Literary Device

Ellison merges fact and fiction again in this chapter, as the image of the narrator speaking on behalf of women's rights recalls the role abolitionist Frederick Douglass played in the late nineteenth-century Women's Suffrage Movement. Lauded as one of the strongest advocates for women's suffrage, Douglass eventually withdrew his support for the movement when he realized that white women were quick to dismiss the struggle for racial equality once they realized it might undermine support for women's suffrage.

The ease with which the narrator allows himself to be seduced by Hubert's wife again indicates his naiveté. He doesn't stop to think how getting involved with a white woman will affect his credibility, not to mention his safety. Despite his reckless behavior, the narrator is becoming somewhat less self-centered and possibly even more compassionate. Learning that Brother Tod Clifton is missing, the narrator immediately forgets about his own problems.

Glossary

Dick Tracy   comic strip popular during the 1940s and 50s that featured a private detective who always got his suspect.

Paul Robeson   American actor and singer (1898–1976) who was the first black actor to play Othello on Broadway with a white supporting cast. He is perhaps best known for his powerful renditions of black spirituals and working-class folk songs such as "Old Man River." His career was eventually destroyed because of his controversial political stance and his outspokenness against racial injustice.

Chapters 20–21

Summary

Searching for Brother Clifton and Brother Maceo, one of his best contacts and a regular at Barrelhouse's Jolly Dollar who has been missing for some time, the narrator is shocked to find Brother Clifton selling dancing, paper Sambo dolls on a street corner. Without a permit to sell the dolls, Clifton is arrested by a white policeman, who harasses and abuses him. When Clifton strikes back, the policeman shoots and kills Clifton.

Determined to pay tribute to his friend, the narrator organizes a lavish funeral and eulogizes. He also assumes responsibility for informing the neighborhood youth of Brother Clifton's death.

Commentary

These two chapters, which focus on Brother Tod Clifton's death and funeral, mark a major transition in the narrator's character and a pivotal point in the novel, highlighting and illuminating various themes, images, and symbols introduced in previous chapters.

Literary
Device

Ellison uses the scene with the grotesque, dancing dolls to advance the theme of blacks perceived as dolls, puppets, and tokens introduced in Chapter 1 (the "battle royal" scene), in which the boys are forced to scramble for brass tokens on the electrified rug.

Brother Clifton's death has a profound impact on the narrator. For the first time, he becomes emotionally involved with the fate of another human being as he wrestles with his conscience, wondering if there was something he could have said or done to prevent this tragedy. As he recalls his feelings of humiliation and disgust at seeing Brother Clifton selling the Sambo dolls, he may also begin to recall the respect, admiration, and genuine friendship he felt for Brother Clifton prior to seeing him sell the degrading dolls. Thus, his friend's tragic death compels the narrator to examine the meaning of his own life.

Brother Clifton's death also presents the narrator with a complex moral dilemma as he struggles to reconcile his grief with his loyalty to the Brotherhood. (Recall that Jim Trueblood faced a similar moral dilemma as he struggled to reconcile the financial and material needs of his family with his desire to *save face* in the eyes of his community.) According to Brotherhood philosophy, an individual's worth is measured by his or her contributions to the organization. Consequently, because Brother Clifton's outrageous behavior violated the Brotherhood's mission of uplifting the race by working together for the common good of the people, he is no longer worthy of being part of the organization. In the eyes of the Brotherhood, Brother Clifton's behavior is more important than his life, which has little, if any, intrinsic value.

Because the narrator knew Brother Clifton personally, he knows his behavior was totally out of sync with his true character. He also knows that Brother Clifton was not only intelligent but street smart. He knew that by striking a white policeman, he was virtually committing suicide.

Plagued by these troubling thoughts, the narrator realizes that he must make a crucial decision: Will he dismiss his friend's murder as a necessary sacrifice and just another casualty of the race war, or will he honor Brother Clifton's memory and speak out on his behalf? By planning Brother Clifton's funeral and delivering his eulogy, he apparently opts for the latter.

Character Insight

The narrator's decision illustrates his growing emotional maturity, as he is able to separate Brother Clifton's irrational behavior from his essence as a man of principle and integrity and conclude that selling the dolls was totally out of character for him. As he ponders the possible reasons for his friend's behavior, the narrator also begins to examine his own feelings and to think for himself instead of jumping to conclusions and blindly following what others would tell him is *the right thing to do.*

The narrator's newly awakened empathy and compassion are particularly striking compared to his response to Brother Clifton's selling the Sambo dolls, and to his earlier response to Jim Trueblood's story. In both cases, he was appalled by the behavior of a black man. But this time, the narrator identifies with Brother Clifton as a true *blood* (brother) and fellow black man who has been subjected to the same hatred and prejudice he himself has experienced. The narrator did not attempt to analyze Trueblood's situation, but he *does* ask himself what could possibly have prompted Tod Clifton to not only sell the degrading dolls, but to strike a white policeman. He sees that selling the dolls was not a spiteful or ignorant act designed to humiliate the black community. It was a desperate, self-destructive act aimed at expressing his own self-hatred at *selling his people* by being part of an organization that exploits blacks, using them only to advance its own social goals and seeing them as nothing more than dolls or puppets.

Character Insight

Following this line of reasoning, Brother Clifton's striking the white policeman was not the act of an angry, out-of-control man ignorant of the consequences of his actions. It was the deliberate act of a man who has come to a crossroads in his life and realizes he has nothing more to lose. Realizing that Ras was right in accusing him of *selling his people* in exchange for power and recognition from whites, he decides that he can no longer deal with the pressure of living a lie. Reaching the breaking point, he explodes—much like the boiler in the basement of the Liberty Paint Factory—and vents his mental and emotional anguish by selling the dolls, ultimately choosing death over life in a culture that denies him the right to be a man.

Tod Clifton is the "dead man on a cliff" (see "Character Analyses") attempting to live between two conflicting cultures. Unlike Dr. Bledsoe and Rev. Barbee, who seem to have come to terms with their roles as *token* leaders, Brother Clifton refuses to be a puppet. Determined to live his own life, he decides that a life in which he has no control over his own mind and body is not worth living. His fierce desire for freedom is perhaps best expressed in the words of Patrick Henry: "Give me liberty, or give me death!" But while Patrick Henry became renowned as a patriotic American hero, black men such as Tod Clifton and Ras, who exist outside of history, are dismissed as agitators and militants. Brother Clifton's striking the white policeman was not the act of an oppressed American striking a blow for freedom, but a black man attacking the white power structure.

The narrator's funeral oration for Brother Clifton bears some resemblance to Marc Antony's funeral oration for Julius Caesar, who has been murdered by the treacherous Brutus. Hoping to focus the people's attention on Caesar's honorable deeds, Antony proclaims: "The evil that men do lives after them;/the good is oft interred with their bones. . . . " These lines capture the sentiment surrounding Tod Clifton's death. Once applauded as a leader and role model for Harlem's youth, he seems destined to be remembered primarily as the man who sold the Sambo dolls.

But just as Mark Antony tries to reconstruct Caesar's true character, so the narrator attempts to reconstruct Tod Clifton's true character by emphasizing that a man's life should be judged by his cumulative works, not by a single, isolated act. Through his eloquent eulogy, the narrator hopes to instill Brother Clifton's memory in the minds of the people, partly through the frequent repetition of his name. He is also determined not to allow the policeman who killed Brother Clifton to be the one to write his history. By honoring his brother with a lavish funeral, he hopes to establish his legacy.

The narrator realizes that he can function outside the Brotherhood and no longer looks to the organization for his identity or values. His new vision of history as a matter of chance and luck (much like the image of the roulette wheel described by one of the vets at the Golden Day) sets him even farther apart from the Brotherhood, with its focus on history as progress.

Glossary

Peace, it's wonderful! a catch phrase attributed to Father Divine (George Baker, c. 1877–1965), a famous East Coast storefront preacher who became an important advocate for racial justice. He founded his first "heaven," or communal dwelling, in 1919. During the Depression his Peace Mission provided food and housing to thousands of people in Harlem and throughout the U.S.

Chapter 22

Summary

After Brother Clifton's funeral, several Brotherhood committee members, including Brother Jack and Brother Tobitt, confront and chastise the narrator for having organized Brother Clifton's funeral, demanding to know why he felt justified in organizing this event without consulting other members of the Brotherhood.

The narrator tries to explain his actions, but Brother Jack interrupts him repeatedly, comparing him to Napoleon and accusing him of organizing a hero's funeral for a traitor. The narrator tries in vain to make the Brotherhood see that the issue is not whether Brother Clifton was a traitor, but that he was an innocent, unarmed man shot down in cold blood by a policeman. Finally, exasperated with Brother Jack's rhetoric, the narrator taunts him by calling him "the great white father." At this remark, Brother Jack becomes so irate, his glass eye pops out.

At the end of the meeting, Brother Jack instructs the narrator to report to Brother Hambro for additional training. Although the narrator intends to follow his instructions, he realizes that the Brotherhood is not at all the visionary organization he once thought it was. Yet he still feels that the group at least gives some meaning to his life.

Commentary

This chapter, which consists primarily of dialogue, focuses on an argument between Brother Jack, Brother Tobitt, and the narrator over the narrator's role in organizing Brother Clifton's funeral. The three men focus on their differences surrounding four key issues: group loyalty versus personal responsibility; the definition of a traitor; who best knows—and is thus qualified to speak for—the people of Harlem; and the extent to which complete discipline and sacrifice are worthwhile goals.

The narrator contends that he organized the funeral to highlight Brother Clifton's work in the Brotherhood and to give the black community an opportunity "to express their feelings [and] to affirm themselves." He also claims that he acted on his personal responsibility because he was unable to reach any Brotherhood members for guidance. Finally, he asserts that Brother Clifton deserved a funeral and points out that the key issue is not whether he was a traitor, but that he was shot down by a policeman because he was black.

Brother Jack argues that the narrator had no right to organize the funeral on his own, that he was not hired to think, and that he has no right to exercise his personal responsibility because his ultimate responsibility is to the group. His argument echoes Dr. Bledsoe's tirade in Chapter 6, ignoring the narrator's explanation as to why he took Mr. Norton to Jim Trueblood's shack, while chastising him for his behavior. Brother Jack's chastisement of the narrator's use of the phrase "personal responsibility" also recalls the scene following the battle royal: The school superintendent chastises the narrator for his use of the phrase "social equality." In both instances, the narrator is told that he is, in fact, *not* equal and not entitled to act on his own behalf without the sanction of the white community.

Brother Tobitt supports Brother Jack's argument, asking the narrator how he could organize a funeral for a man who disgraced his own people. To emphasize his point, Brother Tobitt reveals that he is married to a black woman, a revelation that he thinks will cause the narrator to see him as someone who understands black people. When the narrator sarcastically asks him whether he acquired his pseudo-Negro status "by immersion or injection," Brother Tobitt is offended and renews his efforts to put the narrator in his place.

The assertion that Brother Clifton was a traitor to his people is especially disturbing to the narrator, who becomes angry when Brother Jack and Brother Tobitt insist on focusing on the Sambo dolls instead of Brother Clifton's murder. The narrator undoubtedly begins to realize that regardless of an individual's intrinsic characteristics, whether that individual is seen as a hero or a traitor depends primarily on the observer's perspective.

Theme

Initially shocked and repulsed by Brother Jack's glass eye popping out, the narrator is surprised to discover that he is the only one who didn't know about the glass eye. In view of Brother Jack's emotional blindness, that he has a glass eye indicates that he has some physical blindness as well. Aware of his lack of vision, the narrator—who once saw Brother Jack as a visionary leader—now sees him as "a little bantam rooster of a man." This image, which builds on the numerous prior references to Brother Jack's red hair, also suggests a cockfight, advancing the theme of men behaving like animals introduced in Chapter 1.

Brother Jack's losing his glass eye also recalls the scene at the Liberty Paint Factory in which Lucius Brockway loses his false teeth. In both instances, the loss of these artificial elements suggests the loss of the false sense of power associated with the two men.

Character Insight

Ironically, while Brother Jack symbolically loses his vision, the narrator begins to see more clearly. In previous chapters, even when others pointed things out, the narrator took an inordinate amount of time to finally see what went wrong. But listening to Brother Jack and Brother Tobitt, the narrator not only hears what they have to say, he also asks probing questions and begins to see the meaning behind their words. He begins to realize that his goals and values—especially as they relate to complete discipline and the group's willingness to sacrifice a member's life for the good of the group—are diametrically opposed to the Brotherhood's goals and values.

The allusion to the Cyclops, a mythical one-eyed monster who threatens Odysseus and his men in Homer's *The Odyssey* as they seek to return to their homeland, is significant. Through his cleverness and cunning, Odysseus outwits the Cyclops and blinds him, enabling his men to escape. If Brother Jack is the Cyclops, the narrator is cast as Odysseus, trying to defeat the monster and find his way home.

Glossary

From your ma   the narrator utters this phrase to "signify" on Brother Jack (engage him in a type of wordplay popular in the black community that generally includes insults aimed at "your mama").

Brutus   Marcus Junius Brutus (c. 85–42 B.C.) Roman statesman and general; one of the conspirators who murdered Julius Caesar.

You're riding 'race' again   equivalent to the contemporary phrase "playing the race card."

Chapter 23

Summary

The narrator returns to Harlem and encounters Ras addressing a crowd that has gathered there to hear him speak against the Brotherhood. Ras sees the narrator, and the two argue briefly. As the narrator walks away, two of Ras's men follow and attack him, but a doorman at a movie theater intervenes on his behalf.

As the narrator waits for a cab, three men wearing dark glasses stand near him on the curb, whom he immediately identifies as Ras's men. Instead of running, the narrator buys himself a pair of dark glasses. From then on, he is mistaken for someone named Rinehart, especially when he adds a wide-brimmed hat to his disguise. Even Brother Maceo and Barrelhouse, the bartender, mistake him for Rinehart at the Jolly Dollar. The narrator marvels at how a hat and dark glasses enable him to hide in plain sight. He also decides to exploit his newfound invisibility.

Remembering his appointment with Brother Hambro, the narrator heads for Manhattan. When he expresses his concern about Ras and his men gaining more control in Harlem, Brother Hambro informs him that there is nothing the Brotherhood can do, as they have decided that the people of the Harlem community must be sacrificed. The narrator protests, pointing out that the Brotherhood has promised to stand by the people of Harlem. But Brother Hambro simply explains that the Brotherhood's plans have changed, that black people need to be "brought along more slowly," and that they cannot be allowed to upset "the master plan." Outraged by Brother Hambro's revelation, the narrator heads back to Harlem.

Walking the streets, the narrator realizes that he has been part of a sellout: He promised his people support, only to betray them. Recognizing that there is no escape from his predicament, he decides to use the Brotherhood's own methods against itself. Remembering his grandfather's words, he decides to "agree them [the members of the Brotherhood] to death and destruction." Wondering what Rinehart would do in his situation, he decides to use a woman. Recalling that Emma was once attracted to him, the narrator decides to use her to get information about the Brotherhood's new plans.

Commentary

Rinehart, whom the reader never actually meets in the novel, is the ultimate trickster and master of disguise. Simply by donning dark glasses and a hat, he easily assumes and discards his multiple identities as preacher, lover, numbers runner, and pimp. In effect, he becomes invisible at will, which enables him to mingle with society and go about his business without feeling compelled to explain his actions to anyone. Compared to all the other characters in the novel whose painful experiences have distorted their perceptions of reality, Rinehart seems virtually unscathed and unaffected by his environment because instead of allowing others to define him and shape his reality, he defines himself and creates his own reality.

If Rinehart appears to be especially devious and deceptive, in reality, he has simply learned to adapt to his environment. People in general play numerous roles throughout their lives—sometimes sisters, brothers, friends, students, workers, etc.—and each role that is played emphasizes certain aspects of the personality. Happiness and success in various areas of a person's life depends on how well the individual can play the part.

Style & Language

As his name suggests, Rinehart is both "rind" and "heart"; that is, he is a whole human being who doesn't need others to validate his existence. When the narrator finally removes his metaphorical blindfold and stops seeing his reflection in the eyes of others, he *becomes* Rinehart and regains his sense of self.

By disguising himself as Rinehart, the narrator uses his invisibility to his advantage. He realizes that just as he never noticed the zoot-suiters or the men in dark glasses before, people never really noticed him before. Instead, they recognized him only by his clothes, but not by his features. When people look at him, they see what they expect to see. Who he is, is not as important as who people *think* he is.

This revelation causes the narrator to reflect on his past, recognizing that he is the sum total of his experiences, and that it is his experiences—not the acceptance or rejection of others—that shape his identity.

One of the most important lessons the narrator learns in this chapter is the fallacy underlying the concept of a *color-blind* society. As he points out, "I had thought they [the members of the Brotherhood] accepted me because they felt that color made no difference, when in reality it made no difference because they didn't see either color or men."

Glossary

like a bad dream of the Fiery Furnace   allusion to the biblical story of Shadrach, Meshach, and Abednego (Daniel 3). After being thrown into a fiery furnace by King Nebuchadnezzar for refusing to worship a golden idol, the three Christians emerged unharmed. References to the fiery furnace signify a punishment that "boomerangs" by harming those who attempt to enforce it instead of the intended victims.

antiphonal   sung or chanted in alternation. The allusion is to a child's game, such as "London Bridge Is Falling Down."

charlatan   a person who pretends to have expert knowledge or skill; a fake.

hobnailed boots   boots with short, broad-headed nails on the soles; in this context, an allusion to Hitler's armies.

a few Pullman porters   allusion to the Brotherhood of Sleeping Car Porters, the first successful black labor union in the U.S.

Chapter 24

Summary

The following day, watching the Harlem community "going apart at the seams," the narrator initiates his plan, telling Brotherhood members whatever he thinks they want to hear. Later that afternoon, he tests the effectiveness of his tactics by announcing that his group has launched a clean-up campaign in Harlem to get the people's minds off Brother Clifton's death. He turns in a fake list of new members, amazed at how easily the Brotherhood accepts his lies.

Giving up on his plan to pursue Emma to get information about the Brotherhood, he pursues Sybil, the wife of a Brotherhood member, instead. But while he thinks he is using Sybil to meet his needs, she uses him to fulfill her sexual fantasy: being raped by a black man.

Following their abortive attempt to have an affair, the narrator puts Sybil in a cab and takes a bus back to Harlem. After getting off the bus and running toward the Harlem neighborhood, the narrator passes underneath a bridge and is forced to use his briefcase as a shield to protect himself from the droppings of pigeons perched on the bridge.

Commentary

The narrator's attempt to have an affair with Sybil, George's sexually frustrated wife, illustrates the uneasy relationships between black men and white women. Sybil, the forbidden fruit, represents the taboo of the white female symbolized by several of the white women in the novel: Hubert's nameless wife; Mr. Norton's nameless daughter; Emma, the sophisticated hostess at the Chthonian; and the naked blonde at the battle royal.

Similarly, representing a strict taboo, the narrator is especially appealing to Sybil. But because Sybil sees the narrator as a racial stereotype, he becomes disinterested.

According to Greek and Roman mythology, Sibyl was a famous prophetess who always told the truth, although no one ever believed her. In this instance, Sybil has obviously lied to her husband George, but she does tell the narrator the truth about her rape fantasies involving black men, whom she perceives primarily as sexual animals. Recalling the chaotic scene at the Golden Day, Sybil's fantasy of black men mirrors Edna's fantasy of white men as over-sexed creatures with "monkey glands."

The mythical Sibyl was also believed to be one of the Sirens whose haunting melodies lured sailors to their death. Perhaps additional connections between the symbolism inherent in Sybil's name and her role in the novel can be made.

Because the narrator is at least somewhat attracted to Sybil and even begins to feel protective towards her—although his initial motive for getting involved with her was to use her to get information—he has been lured by her "siren song." And in light of the screaming sirens in Chapter 25, which add to the confusion and chaos in Harlem, the narrator's disastrous encounter with Sybil foreshadows his disastrous encounter with Scofield and Dupre, the looters who convince him to participate in the riot by burning down the tenement.

An important aspect of this chapter as well as the previous two chapters is the emphasis on heat. The narrator meets with the Brotherhood committee (Chapter 22), Brother Jack admonishes him on several occasions to "Sit down, please, it's hot." In Chapter 23, when the narrator enters the bar, he overhears "a heated argument" over Brother Clifton's shooting. And in this chapter, the narrator tells us that his encounter with Sybil takes place on "a hot dry August night." The *heat* motif suggests that the black community is "heating up," much like a smoldering fire about to burst into flame.

The grotesque scene in which the narrator, walking underneath the bridge, is splattered by bird droppings, recalls an earlier scene in which the narrator watches the mockingbirds on his beloved college campus soil the statue of the Founder, symbolizing the white stain on black history. Here, the narrator, who has finally realized that his experiences shape his identity and that—like his grandfather—he is a part of history, suffers the same fate as the Founder.

Glossary

a crazy Thurber cartoon   allusion to James Thurber (1894–1961), American short-story writer and cartoonist.

a new birth of a nation   allusion to *Birth of a Nation* (originally titled *The Klansman*), often described as one of the most racist films ever made.

the Palisades   a popular New Jersey amusement park, now closed.

Chapter 25

Summary

Running through the streets of Harlem, the narrator is accidentally shot after stumbling into the path of two armed policemen in pursuit of four men stealing a safe. A man later identified as Scofield, stops to help the narrator and discovers that the bullet only "knicked" his head. The narrator's briefcase, apparently misplaced in the melee, is returned to him.

Seeing that one of the men carrying the safe has been killed, the startled narrator realizes his wound could have been fatal. Carrying a large cloth bag, Scofield urges the narrator to go with him. The narrator and Scofield meet up with Scofield's friend Dupre, also carrying a sack. Scofield suggests that the narrator has "loot" in his briefcase, but the narrator replies, "Not much," correcting his misperception.

Continuing to follow Scofield and Dupre, the narrator is caught up in Dupre's plan to burn down a tenement building—despite the protests of Dupre's wife. Running from the burning building, the narrator loses his briefcase again and runs back into the flames to retrieve it. He continues running and suddenly finds himself surrounded by seven hanging dummies, which he at first mistakes for human bodies.

The narrator tries desperately to return to Mary's, but while running from two men with baseball bats, he falls into a manhole and lands in a coal cellar, his refuge and sanctuary. Desperate for light, he burns each of the items in his briefcase, discovering that Brother Jack wrote the letter warning him not to "go too fast." Finally, exhausted, having lost all track of time, he falls asleep and dreams of being castrated by Brother Jack while several of the antagonists he has encountered during his life stand by and watch. Awakening from his nightmare, the narrator realizes he can never return to Mary's or to any other part of his past. Resolving to remain in his cellar, stripped of his illusions, the narrator sees his life with renewed vision and clarity.

Commentary

Literary Device

In his Introduction, Ellison remarks that "war could, with art, be transformed into something deeper and more meaningful than its surface violence," and that one way to accomplish such a transformation is through the "comic antidote" of laughter. In this chapter, merging images of violence and destruction with absurd, comic images—the four men running with the safe; the "thrice hatted" Dupre, who conjures up images of the Mad Hatter in *Alice in Wonderland*; the woman carrying a whole side of a cow on her back; Scofield pulling a quart bottle of Scotch out of his hip pocket, and the grotesquely fat, beer-drinking woman on the Borden's milk wagon—Ellison transforms the Harlem riot into something deeper and more meaningful. Connecting the image of the beer-drinking woman with that of the honey wagon in Chapter 13, creates a surprisingly powerful new image: that for blacks, America is not the land of milk and honey, but the land of milk wagons and honey wagons.

Character Insight

Despite his comic approach, however, Ellison depicts a very real sense of the mob mentality. Like the boiler at the Liberty Paint factory, the people have been under so much pressure, they are ready to explode. Any spark will ignite the flames.

Their behavior is self-destructive: Instead of channeling their anger and frustration and targeting the real enemy—the white power structure—they burn down their own homes. The Harlem riot recalls the riot at the Golden Day: instead of turning on Mr. Norton, the vets attack Supercargo. Similarly, Lottie (Dupre's pregnant wife) pleading with him not to burn down their tenement, recalls a similar scene in Chapter 13: Sister Provo pleads with the city officials not to evict her and her husband.

The key images in this chapter mirror the battle royal in Chapter 1: People behave like animals and blindfolded boys fight a boxing match. The narrator's story, which begins and ends in chaos, has "boomeranged" and come full-circle, affirming his statement that "The end was in the beginning" and advancing the themes of blindness, confusion, and anarchy in a world with no rules or boundaries.

This last chapter also reverses some of the images introduced in Chapter 1. The rioters are now drunk on whiskey and instead of white men wolfing down food at the buffet table, black men and women are looting stores, foraging for food. Instead of brass tokens advertising brand-name cars, the looters seek out brand-name foods and apparel (Wilson bacon, Dobbs hats, Budweiser beer, etc.), which illustrates their physical hunger as well as their psychological hunger to participate in America's consumer-based society. Finally, instead of a naked blonde with a flag tatoo, this chapter presents the absurd image of black boys in blonde wigs.

Advancing the theme of chaos and confusion, this chapter merges several scenes from preceding chapters into the melee of the riot. The looters filling their buckets with coal oil recalls the "Cast Down Your Bucket" speech in Chapter 1, and evokes images of the buckets of white paint at the Liberty Paint Factory and the narrator's hideout in the coal cellar of the "whites only" apartment building.

Theme

The narrator's comment comparing the riot to a Fourth of July celebration is significant. Enslaved Africans had no reason to celebrate the Fourth of July, as Frederick Douglass pointed out in his powerful speech, "What to the Slave is the Fourth of July." From this perspective, the riot is a revolt against victimization and oppression on a day that celebrates freedom for whites.

Also important are Scofield's and Dupre's "cotton picking" sacks, which conjure up images of enslaved black Africans toiling in the cotton fields on countless Southern plantations. During the riot, Dupre uses his sack to carry loot. Dupre's vision—his version of the American Dream—is to fill his sack with $10 bills and return to the South.

Style & Language

Similarly, merging images of the race war and the *riding race* metaphor with horse racing by alluding to horses and riders, Ellison plays on the word "race." The most detailed of these images is that of Ras on his "great black horse." A secondary image is the juxtaposition of the famous racehorse, Man o' War, and the equally famous (but forgotten) jockey, Earle Sande. By introducing these two figures along with the image of The Lone Ranger and his horse, Silver, Ellison points out a dual irony of America's racist society: Not only do Americans remember the horse (Man o' War) but not the jockey (Earle Sande), they are more likely to remember a fictional white character (The Lone Ranger) than a factual black figure (Sande). Finally, from the moment the narrator becomes involved in the riot to the moment he falls down the manhole into the coal cellar, he tries desperately to get back to Mary's, a place that still represents his only source of safety and refuge.

It is only when he finally rids himself of his past by burning the items in his briefcase that he is able to become *whole* in his hole and envision a life without illusion.

Glossary

Men who seemed to rise up out of the sidewalks . . . allusion to the story of Jason and the Argonauts' "Quest of the Golden Fleece." To prove himself worthy of the Golden Fleece, Jason—by order of King Aetes—must sow a field with dragon's teeth, which spring up into a "crop" of armed men and attack him. With the help of Medea, the king's daughter, he defeats the men and escapes with the Golden Fleece.

Joe Louis born Joe Louis Barrow (1914–81); U.S. boxer, world heavyweight champion from 1937 to 1949

t-bees reference to tuberculosis, an infectious lung disease often referred to as TB.

ex post facto done or made afterward.

fusillade a simultaneous or rapid and continuous discharge of many firearms.

Earle Sande (sic) Earl Sande (1898–1968), a black jockey inducted into the Sports Hall of Fame for riding Gallant Fox to horse racing's Triple Crown in 1930.

Man o' War legendary race horse (1917–1947) that set three world records and two American records.

Heigho . . . Silver allusion to *The Lone Ranger*, a TV western popular during the 1940s and 50s.

Epilogue

Summary

In the Epilogue, the narrator speaks to us from his underground hideout again. Having had time to reflect on his life, he has decided that reality exists in the mind.

The narrator considers coming out of hibernation and facing the world once again, reasoning that "even an invisible man has a socially responsible role to play."

Commentary

Resuming his reflections on the meaning of his life that he began in the Prologue, the narrator, having survived numerous traumatic experiences, including the madness of the Harlem riot, can now reflect on his life with a detached objectivity that he was unable to achieve before he realized that, through his imagination, he has the power to transform and transcend reality. He has also achieved a clarity of vision that enables him to see things from a different perspective.

After getting to know him on a more personal level as a unique individual instead of as a nameless, anonymous black man, the reasons behind his ramblings are understandable. Without this knowledge, labeling him "crazy" and simply discounting or dismissing his remarks would be the greater inclination. Recalling the narrator's initial encounter with the veterans at the Golden Day, in light of his own experiences he is likely to be more sympathetic and understanding of their situation at this point in his life than he was as a naïve young college student. Although the world around him has not changed significantly, the narrator's attitude toward life and his perspective concerning normal versus abnormal behavior have changed dramatically, because he is now a *veteran* of the race war.

The narrator's remark regarding his "belated appreciation of the crude joke that had kept me running" reveals his enhanced emotional maturity, as does his struggle to come to terms with the meaning of his grandfather's advice. Despite the torture he has been forced to endure, he is still *stupidly* alive, which suggests that living in a world that denies an individual basic human rights is a fate worse than death. He reiterates his stance, "I'm invisible, not blind."

The narrator's accidental meeting with Mr. Norton in the subway is key. Norton asks him for directions but doesn't recognize him as the young man he once identified as the keeper of his destiny. Given the narrator's life-long search for his true identity, the narrator's realization, which he attempts to share with Mr. Norton, that "if you don't know *where* you are, you probably don't know *who* you are" means that unless an individual understands their place in history, they can never hope to discover their identity.

Concerning his reasons for writing down his story, the narrator realizes that the process of writing helped him work through the pain, diffuse the hate, and regain his capacity to love. Once more, he reflects on the experiences of his grandfather who, even as a slave, never doubted his humanity. In the final analysis, the narrator suggests that even though his experiences as a black man in white America are unique, his experiences have much in common with the experiences of all human beings. He suggests that even though he speaks on his own behalf, perhaps on some level, he speaks for each of us.

Whether the narrator is seen as hero or victim depends on whether he is seen literally living underground or as metaphorically living in his subconscious—whether to believe that he is hibernating or whether to assume that he is merely hiding. In his essay "Change the Joke and Slip the Yoke," Ellison is quite emphatic about the meaning of the novel's closing scene. As he points out, the narrator's movement down into "a coal cellar, a source of heat, light, power" is not an act of "concealment in darkness"; it is "a process of rising to an understanding of his human condition."

Glossary

heart of darkness   allusion to Joseph Conrad's novel *Heart of Darkness*, published in 1902, which centers on the cruelty of colonial exploitation in the Belgian Congo. The "heart of darkness" is the jungle and the primitive, subconscious human heart.

CHARACTER ANALYSES

The Narrator 88

Mr. Norton 89

Dr. A. Hebert Bledsoe 90

Rev. Homer A. Barbee 91

Jim Trueblood 92

Ras the Exhorter 93

Mary Rambo 94

Brother Tod Clifton 95

Brother Jack 96

The Narrator

The narrator represents a classic case of the "mis-educated Negro," taught to despise his own people—taught a version of American history so thoroughly *whitewashed*, he learned nothing about the countless contributions of black Americans and he has no concept of black history. Rendered invisible due to distortion and lack of documentation in U.S. history texts, taught to accept the myth of white supremacy as fact, the narrator is determined to distance himself from uneducated Southern blacks, to whom he feels vastly superior.

The extent to which the narrator internalized this debilitating myth is best illustrated in Chapter 5. Discovering the actual contents of Bledsoe's letters, the narrator is devastated to learn that the man he trusted and idolized betrayed him and ruined his opportunity for obtaining a college education and a better life. The worst insult the narrator can think of to hurl at him is not *liar* or *traitor*, but "chitterling eater."

Comparing this to his earlier expulsion from college, the narrator learned his lessons well. The worst insult Bledsoe can think of to convey his outrage and hostility is "nigger." By hurling this racial slur at the narrator, Bledsoe reveals his own self-hatred, which he passes on to the narrator. In this way, he perpetuates the racist stereotypes of whites who see blacks as inferior, subhuman creatures.

The narrator represents the classic naïve young man, unlearned in the ways of the world. Although he thinks of himself as educated, the narrator has simply accepted and internalized the ideas and values taught to him by others, which he accepts without question. Unable to question or to seek his own answers to complex issues and lacking a sense of identity or a definitive value system, the narrator does not have a clear sense of who he is and how he fits into society, nor does he possess the intellectual curiosity required to ask the right questions. Similarly, the narrator has not developed a clear self-image, nor does he have the self-confidence to challenge authority figures such as Bledsoe and Norton, whom he perceives to be in control of his fate.

Throughout the novel, the narrator grows from blind ignorance to enlightened awareness as he begins to listen with an open mind, to question, and to draw connections between the experiences of others and his own life. Relating to Brother Tod Clifton's predicament as Clifton wrestles with his conflicting desires to be a leader in the Brotherhood and to be faithful to his black community, the narrator becomes aware of his own internal conflicts.

The grandfather, the narrator's spiritual guide, represents the ancestral shadow of slavery that still haunts contemporary African Americans. According to those who knew him, the grandfather was "the meekest of men," who believed in Booker T. Washington's conciliatory approach that, for the black man, humility is the way to progress and success. The grandfather epitomized the kind of humble, subservient black man often referred to as an "Uncle Tom." But after spending his whole life masking his feelings of hate for the whites who forced him to live a life of degradation and humiliation, he vows that his children and grandchildren must know the truth. The grandfather, on his deathbed, tries desperately to tell them that by adopting a stance of humility and pretending to "go along to get along," they are complicitors in their own destruction.

Describing his grandfather's death, the narrator notes that, after his shocking revelation that he was a traitor to his race, the old man seemed more alive in death than he had ever been in life. Thus the grandfather's spirit lives on, sporadically manifesting itself through other black men who try to provide guidance to the narrator. The narrator *sees* his grandfather's face in other men—the vet, Brother Tarp, and even in the portrait of Frederick Douglass. Therefore, the grandfather continues to guide his grandson throughout his painful and perilous journey towards enlightenment.

Mr. Norton

Mr. Norton represents the white Northern liberal who considers it his duty to *civilize* blacks. Bearing *the white man's burden*, Norton feels compelled to help and enlighten blacks whom he considers as a class of childlike, inferior people, lacking the skills and intelligence to help themselves, and needing a "great white father" to show them the way out of their dark and primitive world.

Norton's patronizing, paternalistic attitude, coupled with a guilty conscience over the role his ancestors played, promoting and perpetuating the slavery system, is a demonstration of what prompts financial contributions to the narrator's black college, exclusive of any genuine interest in or concern for individual blacks.

Although he appears to be a sincere, generous man, Norton is simply a new breed of racist who perpetuates the tradition of exploiting and humiliating blacks, as illustrated by his hundred-dollar donation to Jim Trueblood after listening to his horrific story of incest. Norton's actions are equivalent to those of the Southern white racists at the battle royal who *reward* blacks for abusing each other by tossing them brass tokens. But Norton's tactics are more subtle and covert than those of his Southern counterparts. Although he derives a definite vicarious pleasure from listening to Trueblood's story, Norton can walk away feeling morally superior to this *inferior* man and, by paying him for his story, absolve himself of his guilty social conscience. The covert Northern racist disguised as a liberal philanthropist is even more dangerous than the overt Southern racist who makes no attempt to hide his hatred of blacks. Both promote and perpetuate negative behavior among blacks—from the Bledsoes to the Truebloods—rewarding them for *playing the nigger*. Bledsoe and Trueblood are separated by class, but they share the common bond of race. Both their names evoke images of blood: blood ties (the brotherhood of black men) or bloodshed (the brutalities of slavery).

Dr. A. Hebert Bledsoe

Instead of preserving and protecting the legacy of the Founder, Dr. Bledsoe distorts and perverts the Founder's dream of lifting the veil of ignorance from his people. Rather than enlightening his students and providing them with an education that prepares them to contribute to society and function as educated adults in the real world, Bledsoe perpetuates the myth of white supremacy. Thus, pondering the statue of the Founder lifting the veil, the narrator suspects that Bledsoe is, in fact, lowering the veil and ensuring that his students remain *in the dark*. Bledsoe tells the narrator, who sees education as a means of achieving a sense of pride and dignity, "You let the white folk worry about pride and dignity—you learn where you are and get yourself power, influence, contacts with powerful and influential people—then stay in the dark and use it!" Like the mockingbird that befouls the statue of the Founder, Bledsoe makes a mockery of the Founder's dream.

Although he appears to be everything that Rev. Barbee is not, Bledsoe is a mirror image of Rev. Barbee. Seeing Rev. Barbee on stage in the auditorium for the first time, the narrator has a hard time distinguishing between the two men, both of whom are fat, bald, and ugly.

Bledsoe also shares the Reverend's mannerism of "making a cage of his fingers" as he talks and, like the Reverend, he carries a white handkerchief (but his is embroidered in blue).

Considering the controversies that surrounded Booker T. Washington, regarded by some as a respected black leader and by others as a "sellout" and "Uncle Tom" for his conservative views on social equality for blacks, Barbee and Bledsoe represent two contrasting views of Washington, the model for the Founder.

Like Trueblood, Bledsoe is a blues singer and storyteller, but he is also an egotist and a power-hungry opportunist. From Barbee's sermon, Bledsoe was once an idealistic young man like the narrator who truly believed in the Founder's dream, but his painful experiences as a black man in a racist white society so distorted his vision of what his life could be that he can no longer see the dream. As Barbee points out, he is unable to reconcile the way things are with the way they're supposed to be; he can no longer cope with the brutal reality of his life. To survive, he learned to *play the game* at the expense of killing his soul and betraying his people.

Bledsoe apparently feels that to disillusion the narrator and tell him the truth about the narrator's perceived role in society is better than allowing him to discover it for himself. But the narrator refuses to listen to Bledsoe and threatens to expose him. Realizing he can no longer control him, Bledsoe devises a devious plot to get rid of the narrator before he can cause trouble for the school.

Rev. Homer A. Barbee

Like his namesake (Homer, author of *The Odyssey* and *The Iliad*), Rev. Homer A. Barbee is a blind poet and storyteller who keeps the past alive through songs and stories. Rev. Barbee is the down-home Southern preacher transplanted to the North. Although he hails from Chicago, Barbee has not lost touch with his southern roots. Barbee preaches his sermon about the Founder in the college auditorium with all the fervor and flair of the traditional black preacher addressing his congregation from the pulpit of a small Southern church where the service was often followed by a barbecue: the congregation, having been spiritually nourished by *the Word*, continued their fellowship by enjoying the food lovingly prepared by the church ladies.

Barbee's blindness is significant for several reasons. Unlike Bledsoe, whose primary concern is ensuring that the evening's *performance* is appropriate for his distinguished white guests, Barbee is totally unaware of the whites in the audience and directs his message to the black congregation, revealing that he was not always blind. In his mind's eye, he still sees the college the way it was in the "old days" when his fiery sermons would evoke a passionate response from his congregation in the form of shouts and "amens." But here, the only response to his sermon is a stiffly polite silence from a new generation of young, educated blacks, taught that singing and shouting in church is uncivilized and undignified. An old woman, overwhelmed by emotion, spontaneously responds to the sermon, but quickly becomes silent, realizing that her outburst is out of place in this modern, progressive (and seemingly enlightened) congregation.

Barbee's physical blindness also symbolizes blacks who view religion as an escape from reality, choosing to remain blind to issues facing them in the real world. It also symbolizes those who, like Bledsoe, have become spiritually blind, counting on their *god* of material wealth and power to save them.

Barbee represents the type of Southern black preacher the students have been taught to despise by people like Dr. Bledsoe. Ironically, he commands their respect because he is from Chicago.

Jim Trueblood

Although to think of him as the ignorant, illiterate sharecropper, committing incest with his teenage daughter, is the greater tendency, Jim Trueblood is neither ignorant nor illiterate, as illustrated by the meticulous plan he devises to keep from being forced to uproot his family, give up his home, and abandon his land. Despite his behavior, Trueblood emerges as a complex, dignified man who deserves our respect and compassion.

Before he became the subject of vicious gossip, Trueblood was known as a hard worker and a blues singer. Trueblood's singing symbolizes his spiritual strength, which enables him to survive his ordeal by accepting responsibility for his behavior and praying for forgiveness. Once he has worked through this painful healing process, Trueblood regains his ability to sing. With his soul cleansed and his spirit renewed, Trueblood returns to his family, seeks their forgiveness, and works to make the best of their tragic situation. After carefully considering his options and weighing the consequences, Trueblood refuses to allow his wife and daughter to obtain abortions, concluding that killing two innocent babies would only compound his sin. Thus, Trueblood demonstrates that his first priority is caring for his family, not seeking the approval of a judgmental community.

Trueblood is also a shrewd man who understands the workings of the white power structure, manipulating it to his advantage. After receiving his eviction notice from the college, he refuses to uproot his family and give up his home. Realizing that he has no chance of openly challenging Bledsoe, Trueblood appeals to his boss, Mr. Buchanan, who writes a letter to Sheriff Barbour on his behalf, describing his situation. When the sheriff along with some other men, after listening to Trueblood's story, reward Trueblood with food, drink, and tobacco, instead of condemning him, Trueblood realizes that he can use his story to his advantage. Although Trueblood is initially shocked to discover that his pain and suffering is a source of entertainment for the white men, he quickly learns to take advantage, using their morbid fascination with his sexual behavior for his own benefit. Once he learns that he can profit from his pain, Trueblood embellishes his story with detail and dialogue, creating the elaborate version he shares with Norton. Trueblood is aware of his story's impact on whites and exploits them to get their money, which ultimately improves his family's living conditions. Although Trueblood is a victim, he is also a trickster, gaining some power over whites and using it to his own advantage.

Ras the Exhorter

The character of Ras is reminiscent of Bigger Thomas, the protagonist of Richard Wright's *Native Son*, often referred to as the ultimate protest novel. (See "Introduction to the Novel" for more on the relationship between Wright and Ralph Ellison.) Like Bigger, Ras is eventually "propelled into violence by overwhelming conditions and forces." But unlike Bigger, Ras is not a rash young man who acts out of panic and fear; he is a rational, thinking man, whom the narrator compares to a king and a general. Subjected to constant pressure with no release, he finally *explodes* much like the overloaded boiler in the Liberty Paint Factory.

But Ras is also a visionary and a prophet. Ras's message, like that of essayist Ralph Waldo Emerson, is "Self-Reliance." But because Ras is black, he is perceived not as a visionary and leader, but as a dangerous militant and rabble-rouser whose voice must be silenced. He is the only black man in the novel who chooses and then changes his own name. But because he has "stepped outside of history," Ras is perceived as a crazy, ridiculous figure. Instead of seeing him as a general and leader, the inclination is to dismiss him as a black *Don Quixote*, fighting windmills. Ras does, however, have powerful oratory skills—he nearly convinces Brother Clifton that he has joined the wrong "Brotherhood" and is "selling his people," which eventually leads to tragic consequences for the charismatic young man he acknowledges as his "black prince."

Ras is modeled after Marcus Garvey (1887–1940), a renowned Black Nationalist and founder of the United Negro Improvement Association (UNIA), a forerunner of the NAACP (National Association for the Advancement of Colored People). Garvey, a Jamaican immigrant, believed that blacks would never achieve social, political, and economic equality in the United States. He launched the "Back to Africa" movement popular during the 1940s aimed towards helping blacks return to Mother Africa. Aided by whites, who agreed with his vision of a separate black nation, Garvey founded the Black Star shipping line and prepared to transport blacks back to Africa. Before he was able to carry out his plan, he was indicted for mail fraud and imprisoned for two years, and then deported to Jamaica. Although Garvey continued his racial advocacy, he was unable to recapture the momentum of his project, which ultimately failed. Ironically, few Americans recognize Garvey's philosophy echoed Emerson's philosophy of self-reliance.

Mary Rambo

As her name suggests, Mary Rambo is both Mary, the saintly mother of Jesus, and Aunt Jemima, the female version of Sambo. Mary is a strong black woman who has learned to survive the violence and corruption of the city by relying on her inner resources. A Southern woman who now lives in the North, Mary provides the narrator's only source of love and comfort.

After his harrowing experience at the Liberty Paint Factory Hospital, the narrator is grateful for Mary's kindness and generosity. Seeing him simply as a fellow human being who needs help, Mary takes him into her home, cooks for him, and nurses him back to health. When he can't pay his rent, she tells him not to worry. Seeing how depressed he is about his situation, Mary encourages him and reassures him that he will make something of himself and be "a credit to his race." She does everything she can to demonstrate her faith in him and, in effect, adopts him as her surrogate son.

During this time, the narrator sees Mary as the saintly mother figure, referring to her as his anchor and guide, and appreciating her support and generosity. But after he meets Brother Jack and begins to work for the Brotherhood, he sees Mary through different eyes. She becomes a source of shame and embarrassment for him, prompting him to try to *shatter her image*, as symbolized by his futile attempt to discard the cast-iron bank. The bank, like Mary, represents a part of his heritage he wants to forget. Although he initially appreciates her cooking, he now complains of his steady diet of cabbage. At first he sees her home as a sanctuary and source of solace and comfort, but later he notices the noise, poverty, and filth surrounding her, as indicated by the banging on the pipes, the smell of cabbage, and the invasion of roaches.

He finally leaves Mary without even saying goodbye, confident that she will survive, having undoubtedly gone through similar experiences with other black men.

Mary is a survivor who represents the courage and dignity of the black woman. Although she is not based on any specific historical character, she is a woman in the tradition of Harriet Tubman, Sojourner Truth, or Mary McCloud Bethune.

Brother Tod Clifton

Tod Clifton (whose first name in German means "dead") is the handsome, articulate young brother assigned as Harlem's Youth Leader. Although the narrator first considers him a competitor, he soon realizes that Tod is not interested in political power; he sincerely wants to help the youth of Harlem break out of their limited reality and realize their unlimited potential. Because Tod is one of the most charismatic characters in the novel, it is difficult to reconcile his act of selling Sambo dolls and his violent death with his *true* character.

Tod Clifton, the sensitive, idealistic young man with his black skin and "Afro-Anglo-Saxon" features, may be portrayed as the man on a cliff who, devastated by the violence and hatred that surround him, is finally pushed over the edge and, in effect, commits suicide by striking the white policeman who arrests him for selling the dolls without a permit.

Tod Clifton's emotional reaction to Ras's speech concerning the black man's place in white America, illustrates that he is a highly impressionable young man. Although he wants to dismiss Ras as a fanatic rabble-rouser, Tod knows that Ras speaks the truth, which causes him to question his effectiveness with his youth group. When Ras accuses him of *selling his people*, he realizes that he has *sold out* to the Brotherhood. Unable to reconcile his idealistic vision with his reality and unwilling to compromise his ideals, he gives up, choosing death rather than life without hope, respect, or dignity. Similarly, while Ras wants to dismiss Tod as an opportunist who has *sold out* to the system, he recognizes him as *a black prince* and spares his life.

Brother Jack

In the character of Brother Jack, Ellison merges the trickster of black folklore with the trickery and deceptiveness of whites toward blacks. According to black folklore, Jack (or John) is the great human culture hero who usually defeats "Ole Massa, God and the Devil."

As symbolized by his single eye, Jack is partially blind and sees blacks only as a group, not as individuals. His one eye also conjures up the image of the Cyclops, the one-eyed creatures who capture Odysseus' men. Considering the theme of games and gaming, Jack is not, as the narrator remarks at one point, one of "the kings of the earth;" he is simply a One-Eyed Jack, a wild card whose value depends on the game being played.

CRITICAL ESSAYS

Symbols and Symbolism in
Invisible Man 98

Wordplay in *Invisible Man* 102

Profiles of Leadership in
Invisible Man 104

Harlem: City of Dreams 107

Symbols and Symbolism in *Invisible Man*

A master of poetic devices, Ralph Ellison incorporates numerous symbols and *archetypes* (universal symbols) into his novel, each providing a unique perspective on the narrative and supporting the dominant themes of invisibility and identity. Dreams and visions generally symbolize the power of the subconscious mind. In the novel, numerous dreams and visions symbolize the narrator's retreat from reality, seeking solace in memories of his childhood or days at the college, often occurring as he escapes into his music. Ellison merges dreams and reality to underscore the surrealistic nature of the narrator's experience and to highlight the gross disparities between the realities of black life and the myth of the American Dream.

Several key symbols enhance *Invisible Man's* overall themes: The narrator's calfskin briefcase symbolizes his psychological baggage; Mary Rambo's broken, cast-iron bank symbolizes the narrator's shattered image; and Brother Tarp's battered chain links symbolize his freedom from physical as well as mental slavery. Other symbolism can generally be divided into four categories: colors, numbers, animals, and machines (humans depicted as dolls, puppets, or robots).

Color Symbolism

Ellison uses color to convey the novel's themes and motifs throughout the book, consistently weaving references to the following colors into the text:

Gold. Gold symbolizes power, elusive wealth, or the illusion of prosperity. References to gold and variations thereof include: the Golden Day, an ironic commentary on the lives of the veterans who, instead of looking forward to their golden years of retirement, escape only once a week on a *golden day* from the mental hospital; the brass tokens, which the boys mistake for gold coins; and the naked blonde's hair, described as "yellow like a Kewpie doll's." Yellow also alludes to light and enlightenment.

Red. Red, often associated with love and passion as in red roses, generally symbolizes blood, rage, or danger in the novel. Brother Jack's red hair (which, along with his blue eyes and white skin, underscore his all-American identity), the red-faced men at the battle royal, the vet's red wheelchair (underscoring his courage), and the frequent references to Santa Claus as a symbol of evil are part of a *red* motif that accents unpleasant personalities and symbolizes the narrator's uneasiness evoked by these characters. Numerous references to red, white, and blue—the white men at the battle royal with their blue eyes and red faces—mock the principles of life, liberty, and the pursuit of happiness symbolized by the Stars and Stripes.

Black/White. Ellison makes several profound statements about American society and the language of racism (white generally symbolizes goodness and purity, while black symbolizes evil and corruption) by reversing traditional black/white symbolism and its associated *white-is-right* philosophy. Black is generally portrayed as good and positive (black skin, Ras's "magnificent black horse," and the "black powerhouse"). White is associated with negative images of coldness, death, and artifice: snow, the white blindfolds, the white fog, the images of a mysterious "white death," the "cold, white rigid chair" at the factory hospital, the optic white paint produced at the Liberty Paint Factory, and Brother Jack's "buttermilk white" glass eye. However, in keeping with Ellison's tendency to reject polar opposites, this symbolism is sometimes reversed: the fragrant white magnolias and the narrator's favorite dessert, vanilla ice cream with sloe gin.

Blue. Blue alludes to the blues, a form of African American folk music characterized by lyrics that lament the hardships of life and the pain of lost love. In the novel, the blues are characterized by Louis Armstrong's "What Did I Do to Be So Black and Blue?" The song haunts the narrator throughout the narrative. The blues motif is also emphasized through frequent references to musical instruments, blues language (exemplified in the excerpts from black folk songs such as "Poor Robin") and references to blues singers such as Bessie Smith and to characters in the novel who sing the blues, such as Jim Trueblood and Mary Rambo. Focusing on the harsh realities of life that black men and women such as Jim and Mary overcome through their strong religious beliefs and unwavering faith that tomorrow will be a better day, Ellison's novel provides a literary counterpart to the blues. The blues provides a musical counterpart to Ellison's novel. References to the color blue also include the blues-singing cart-man's discarded blueprints, the white men's blue eyes, and the naked blonde's eyes, "as blue as a baboon's butt."

Gray. Like white, gray (a slang term used by blacks to refer to whites) is generally associated with negative images. Examples include gray smoke, the dull gray weathered cabins in the former slave quarters, and the gray tinge in the white paint at the paint factory, which symbolizes the bland and homogenous result of mixing black and white cultures without respecting the unique qualities of each. Gray is also alluded to in the fog that greets the narrator upon his arrival at the paint factory, which casts a gloomy and dismal shadow over the landscape and foreshadows the narrator's horrific experiences at the factory and factory hospital.

Green. Although generally associated with nature, in the novel, green is the color of the lush campus verdure and money, the narrator's main motivator.

While Ellison's images of the South are alive with colors of nature—green grass, red clay roads, white magnolias, purple and silver thistle—his images of the North are painted primarily in shades of gray and white. Thus, color contrasts the rural South with its farms and plantations, providing people a means of living off the land, against the urban North, depicted as cold, sterile, and inhospitable.

Number Symbolism

Number symbolism is common in mythology and the Bible, from which Ellison draws many of his symbols and images. The following numbers are especially significant throughout the novel:

Three. Three is widely regarded as a divine number. Many myths and religions have triads of hero-gods: the ancient African deities Ogun, Obatala, and Sango; the Greek gods Zeus, Hera, and Poseidon; and the Christian Trinity of Father, Son, and Holy Spirit. The universe moves through three cycles (growth, dissolution, and redemption) which mirror the three phases of the life cycle (birth, life, and death). In Greek and Roman mythology, the heroic quest consists of three stages (departure, initiation, and return). In the European worldview, time is divided into three parts: past, present, and future, but according to the African worldview, reality consists of three worlds: the worlds of the ancestors, the living, and the unborn. In the novel, the number three occurs at several key incidents: Waiting to give his speech on "Dispossession" at the sports arena, the narrator sees three white mounted policemen on three black horses. He notices three brass rings among Brother and Sister Provo's possessions. Trying to escape from Ras's men, he sees "three men in natty cream-colored summer suits . . . wearing dark glasses."

Seven. Seven signifies completeness and perfection: seven wonders of the ancient world, seven seas, and seven ages of man. According to the Bible, God created the world in seven days. Biblical scholars also refer to the seven last words of Christ, meaning the seven last sentences Christ allegedly uttered, compiled from all the Gospels. According to the Jewish religion, there are seven heavens, of which the seventh is the place of God. In his classic book, *The Souls of Black Folk*, W.E.B. Du Bois refers to "the Negro" as "the seventh son." In the novel, Dr. Bledsoe gives the narrator seven letters addressed to seven prospective employers. By focusing on the number seven, Ellison underscores Du Bois' statement, highlighting the narrator's experiences as symbolizing the experiences of black men in white America.

Twelve. Twelve, like seven, symbolizes completeness and perfection. But in African American folklore, the number twelve also refers to *playing the dozens*—a wordplay ritual that often involves insulting one's mother.

Animal Symbolism

Animal symbolism pervades the novel. Men, referred to as snakes, dogs, horses, and oxen, mirror the violent, chaotic world of the twentieth century, in which humans (primarily men) often behave like animals. The animal symbolism in the Northern scenes also underscores the images of life as a circus and New York as a zoo.

Machine Symbolism

Through frequent references to "the man in the machine" (the first occurs in Chapter 2, where Trueblood dreams that he is trapped inside the clock), Ellison emphasizes the stark contrasts between the agricultural South, with its farms and plantations, and the industrial North, with its factories and steel structures. This image is particularly powerful in Chapters 11 and 12, which focus on the Liberty Paint Factory and the factory hospital. The narrator is trapped inside the glass and metal box. In the final dream sequence, the bridge (the "machine") *becomes* a man and walks away. Machine symbolism emphasizes the destruction of the individual by industry and technology, highlighting the lack of empathy and emotion in a society where people are indifferent to the needs of others.

Wordplay in *Invisible Man*

Ellison obviously delights in wordplay to achieve what he describes as blues-toned laughter. One of the more fascinating aspects of the novel, Ellison's wordplay—allusions, puns, and rhymes as well as powerful metaphors and similes—adds a dimension of literary and cultural richness to the novel.

Ellison bases much of his wordplay on *black vernacular*, the ordinary language of black Americans, enriched by colloquial expressions and proverbs as well as excerpts from songs and stories rooted in African and African American culture. *Vernacular* refers to the native form of ordinary language, as opposed to the literary or learned forms. Vernacular includes pronunciation and local dialect. A *faucet* on the West Coast is a *spigot* on the East Coast, while *heavy traffic* in the Midwest becomes *gridlock* in California.

In Chapter 25, Dupre, providing instructions for burning down the tenement building, warns, "After that it's every tub on its own black bottom!" Ellison might have used the more common and less colorful phrase, *After that it's every man for himself*, but this would not have grounded the scene in black culture. The two winos use a vivid simile to describe Ras on his horse, "looking like death eating a sandwich." A third example is Trueblood's play on the word *whippoorwill*: "we'll whip ole Will when we find him."

Ellison achieves much of his comic effect through a unique form of wordplay called *playing the dozens*. Rooted in black vernacular, playing the dozens is a subversive type of wordplay in which the oppressed (blacks) use the language of the oppressor (whites) against them without directly confronting or openly challenging the oppressor. Ranging from mildly insulting to overtly obscene, playing the dozens is a coded language that uses puns, hyperbole, humor, irony, repetition, reversal, and understatement to score points, and often includes sexual innuendo and references to "your mama." Following are some examples of this type of wordplay in the novel:

Puns. *Puns* involve a word or words that sound alike in order to juxtapose, connect, or suggest two or more possible applications of the word or words, usually in a humorous way: trigger/nigger, Ras/race, yam/I am, trusties/trustees, Monopolated/manipulated, exhorter/extorter, homburg/humbug, Rambo/Sambo, and taboo/tatoo. Other examples include plays on characters' names, such as Wrestrum (restroom), Tobitt (two-bit), and Tatlock (deadlock). In the end, the narrator becomes whole in his hole.

Hyperbole. *Hyperbole* is an extreme exaggeration used for effect and not meant to be taken literally: *He's as strong as an ox; I've told you a million times.* . . . . Examples in the novel include Scofield pulling a quart bottle of Scotch out of his hip pocket and the woman carrying a whole side of beef on her back.

Humor. Ellison coins new terms and creates his own language. Having established the traits and eccentricities of a character, the character's name conveys a certain action or activity. Examples include "Bledsoing," referring to his sunglasses as "Rineharts" and expressing his intent to "out-Tobitt Tobitt."

Irony. *Irony* involves expressing the opposite of what one believes to be true. Examples of irony include the narrator's desire to follow in Dr. Bledsoe's footsteps, which he ultimately does, even though he is expelled from college; the narrator's desire to see Dr. Bledsoe exposed as a "chitterling eater," when he himself is so exposed by the drunk at the Chthonian; and the image of Mary's bank *exploding*, shortly after the narrator tells us that his head is about to explode. The ultimate irony is that the Invisible Man, obsessed with the blindness of others, is blinded. He refuses to see the truth even when others point it out to him.

Repetition. The refrain of the line "What Did I Do to Be So Black and Blue?" as well as various takes on the song "Poor Robin" ("They picked poor robin clean") and numerous references to "buckets" in a variety of contexts, ranging from the metaphorical buckets in Booker T. Washington's "Cast Down Your Bucket" speech to paint buckets at the Liberty Paint Factory and buckets of coal oil at the Harlem Riot, all provide examples of repetition.

Reversal. The novel presents images of inverted reality as well as numerous reversals: black is white, dark is light, freedom is bondage, and underground is aboveground. Trying to elevate himself above others whom he considers beneath him, the narrator becomes involved with the Brotherhood, eventually causing his downfall.

Understatement. Understatement involves depicting a scene or describing an image in weaker terms than warranted by truth, accuracy, or importance, thereby underscoring its importance. Trueblood's simple understatement, "I was lost" to describe his sexual feelings towards his daughter, is a key example.

Other examples of wordplay include *oxymorons* ("[T]he darkness of lightness" and "The end is in the beginning") and *double entendres*. The blindfolds described as "broad bands" could also refer to radio waves. The word *party* could be interpreted as a social event or a political party in Brother Jack's comment to the narrator, "It's a party, you might like it." And, of course, the novel contains various plays on the word *race*, which include racism, horse races, running, and the human race. Numerous *allusions* to biblical, literary, and historical events are significant because they allude to the strength enslaved black Americans found in their folk culture, history, and religion, enabling them to survive the horrors of slavery.

Ellison's language of music and war supports his underlying themes: the power of music (especially jazz and blues), and America's continuing race war.

Achieving powerful effects, Ellison simply varies the spelling of certain words. Indicated in Chapter 25, referring to the boys in blond wigs, he uses the feminine spelling of *blonde*, linking the image to that of the naked blonde in Chapter 1. Perhaps the subtlest example of this tactic is spelling *briefcase* as *brief case*. By varying the spelling of this word, Ellison not only draws attention to the briefcase itself; he also alerts us to the narrator's story about his experiences as a black man in white America, represented by a *brief case* (an abbreviated argument) for racial justice and social equality.

Profiles of Leadership in *Invisible Man*

Are leaders made, or are they born? Considering the various types of black leaders portrayed in *Invisible Man*, this conundrum that has puzzled scholars throughout the ages raises questions regarding the unique qualities that define black leadership, as opposed to those that define leadership in general.

Invisible Man portrays numerous profiles of black leaders and leadership styles. While some are based on historical figures (such as Booker T. Washington, Louis Armstrong, and Marcus Garvey), others are based on character *types* such as the powerful black Southern preacher (Rev. Homer A. Barbee) and the black educator (Dr. Bledsoe). In his speech at West Point, describing the writing process for *Invisible Man*, Ellison states that he was "concerned with the nature of leadership," and by the lack of effective black leaders in America. Examples of various leadership roles explored throughout the novel that illustrate some of the issues involved in developing effective black leaders follow. In each case, the individuals who assume these leadership roles are limited by society, which consistently reminds them not to "go too fast." Also, the narrator assumes several of these roles as he undergoes his gradual transformation from "ranter to writer."

The Athlete/Entertainer. The athlete/entertainer provides hope for the community by capturing the people's imagination and demonstrating through his own success that, despite the seemingly dismal state of affairs, a better world is possible. This type of leader was exemplified in real life by Jack Johnson, Joe Louis, Louis Armstrong, Bessie Smith, and Paul Robeson. In the novel, Tod Clifton (the prizefighter) throws carefully calculated jabs and punches at Ras in Chapter 9, and Tatlock and Supercargo, attempting to use their physical strength to deal with their environment, characterize the athlete/entertainer.

The Educator. Raised on the philosophy that education is the key to success and opportunity, the educator is best exemplified by figures such as Booker T. Washington and W.E.B. Du Bois. While Washington believed in practical education for the masses, Du Bois believed that education should be reserved for an elite "Talented Tenth" of the black population, who should dedicate themselves to learning the higher arts, such as literature, poetry, and philosophy. He believed that the members of this elite group of educated men and women must then assume the responsibility for educating their brothers and sisters. In the novel, the educator is represented primarily by Dr. Bledsoe who represents a distortion of both models, as he is primarily interested in maintaining his position of prominence at the college, rather than in educating his students to be productive members of society.

The Orator. Convinced that the art of public speaking and the ability to express oneself clearly and eloquently is the key to leadership, the orator is exemplified by figures such as Frederick Douglass and Marcus Garvey. Ras the Exhorter, Homer A. Barbee, and the narrator represent this type of leader in *Invisible Man*.

The Intellectual/Philosopher. Relying on wit and intellect to deal with life's realities, the intellectual/philosopher type, such as W.E.B. Du Bois, is represented in the novel by the cart-man, the bartenders (Big Halley and Barrelhouse), and the vet. In keeping with the novel's sense of *inverted reality*, these characters exemplify the narrator's comment in the Prologue concerning the junkman as a man of vision.

The Preacher. This type of leader relies on his religious beliefs and spiritual strength. Although he sometimes loses sight of reality, he tries to provide his people with a vision of a better world where they will no longer have to bear the pain and suffering of this world. Historical examples of the preacher include Father Divine, Dr. Martin Luther King Jr., and Rev. Jesse Jackson. In the novel, Rev. Homer A. Barbee and the Rev. B.P. Rinehart, "Spiritual Technologist," exemplify *the preacher* leadership.

The Separatist/Black Nationalist. The Black Nationalist believes that integration is not a solution to racism and segregation. Consequently, the only way black people will ever gain respect and equality is to build their own nation. The Black Nationalist stands in violent opposition to the staunch integrationist—represented by Brother Wrestrum—who believes that affiliating himself with a primarily white organization will provide him with a sense of identity, dignity, and security. The most prominent black Nationalist was Marcus Garvey, although groups such as the Nation of Islam and the Black Panthers subscribe to a similar philosophy. In the novel, Ras the Exhorter represents the Black Nationalist philosophy.

The Ancestor. Reminding his people of the courage of their enslaved forebears, the ancestor instills his community with a sense of pride in their cultural and racial heritage. Examples in the novel include the grandfather, the vet, Brother Tarp, and Sister and Brother Provo.

The Token. Also referred to as a "sellout," the token black leader gains his power through the support and approval of whites. Although he appears to be one of the most powerful leaders, as evidenced by his trappings of success (Dr. Bledsoe's two Cadillacs and the narrator's new suit), he is one of the most contemptible and least effective leaders because his leadership depends primarily on his ability to cater to the whims of those who are truly in power.

The Artist/Writer. According to Ellison, the artist/writer is responsible for holding out a vision for society of a better world that is possible only if his audience insists on holding onto their dreams. In the novel, the narrator finally achieves this role when he retires to his underground hideout and, leaving behind the chaos and violence of the external world, finds peace and tranquility in his inner reality. The novel focuses primarily on male leaders, but Ellison also alludes to the power of women, as evidenced by his portrayal of the outspoken West Indian woman at the eviction of Brother and Sister Provo, Sister Provo's determination to return to her house to pray, and Mary Rambo's courage and generosity. In various ways, these women portray the image of the supportive, loving mother who makes it possible for her sons to survive and pursue their dreams of leadership, an image underscored by the narrator's definition of *mother*: "The one who screams when you suffer."

Harlem: City of Dreams

Harlem conjures up visions of the Harlem Renaissance, a cultural revival of black art and literature often associated with literary figures such as Claude McKay, Langston Hughes, and Zora Neale Hurston. Spanning nearly two decades—from the 1920s to the 1940s—the Harlem Renaissance ended with the Harlem Riot of 1943.

Some black artists and scholars, such as Alain Locke, viewed Harlem as a cultural Mecca and saw the Harlem Renaissance as the age of the New Negro because black artists were given an opportunity to define their humanity through their art. But others, such as Richard Wright, saw it as a time when white benefactors, enamored with *primitivism*, supported—and eventually exploited—artists willing to create conventional Negro art. In his essay, "Blueprint for Negro Writing," Wright contends that "New Negro" artists were often perceived by their white benefactors "as though they were French poodles who do clever tricks."

But for the thousands of Southern blacks who came to New York during the Great Migration (1920s to 1940s), Harlem was a City of Dreams. Like the narrator, they were amazed by the freedom urban blacks enjoyed. To Southern sharecroppers, used to working on plantations their forebears worked on as slaves, Harlem's lifestyle must have seemed truly astonishing. But with the poverty of blacks living in crowded, substandard tenements ruled by ruthless landlords, came disillusionment and, like the narrator, Harlem was seen in a different light.

In his essay, "Harlem is Nowhere," Ellison describes living in Harlem as "dwell[ing] in the very bowels of the city [with] "its crimes, its casual violence, its crumbling buildings [and its] vermin invaded rooms. . . ." He also contends that Harlem symbolizes "the Negro's perpetual alienation in the land of his birth."

Ellison often merges fantasy and reality. Based on his experiences living in Harlem, the narrator's struggles are understood. He strives to survive and succeed in the City of Dreams that, for him, became a nightmare.

As the narrator points out, the heart of Harlem is 125th Street, although many of Harlem's social and cultural attractions—the famous Schomburg Center for African American Culture and the Harlem Branch of the YMCA, where both Ellison and Langston Hughes lived during the Harlem Renaissance—are located on 135th Street.

CliffsNotes Review

Use this CliffsNotes Review to test your understanding of the original text, and reinforce what you've learned in this book. After you work through the review and essay questions, identify the quote section, and the fun and useful practice projects, you're well on your way to understanding a comprehensive and meaningful interpretation of *Invisible Man*.

Q&A

1. In the Prologue, the narrator admires the music of:

   a. Ma Rainey

   b. Billie Holiday

   c. Louis Armstrong

   d. Paul Robeson

2. Arriving in Harlem, the narrator is surprised to see:

   a. a group of black people gathered to hear Ras the Exhorter

   b. black girls working at a five-and-dime store

   c. a black policeman directing traffic

   d. all of the above

3. Trying to determine the narrator's identity, the doctors at the factory hospital ask him all of the following questions *except*:

   a. Who was B'rer Rabbit?

   b. Where do you live?

   c. Who is your mother?

   d. What is your name?

4. Brother Tarp gives the narrator a link of chain and:

   a. a portrait of Marcus Garvey

   b. a portrait of Booker T. Washington

   c. a portrait of Frederick Douglass

   d. an old pocket watch

5. Which of the following characters does *not* appear in the narrator's castration dream?

   a. Brother Jack

   b. Brother Tobitt

   c. Mr. Norton

   d. Mr. Emerson

Answers: (1) c. (2) d. (3) b. (4) c. (5) b.

Identify the Quote

Throughout the novel, the narrator is bombarded with advice—much of which he ignores—from people who try to influence his behavior. Match the following "words of wisdom" with the appropriate character:

1. Come out of the fog, young man. And remember you don't have to be a complete fool in order to succeed. Play the game, but don't believe in it—that much you owe yourself. Even if it lands you in a strait jacket or a padded cell. . . .

2. You're a black educated fool, son. These white folk have newspapers, magazines, radios, spokesmen to get their ideas across. If they want to tell the world a lie, they can tell it so well that it becomes the truth; and if I tell them that you're lying, they'll tell the world even if you prove you're telling the truth. Because it's the kind of lie they want to hear. . . .

3. We mean to do right by you, but you've got to know your place at all times.

4. What you trying to deny by betraying the black people? Why *you* fight us? You *young* fellows. You young black men with plenty education; I been hearing your rabble rousing. Why you go over to the enslaver? What kind of education is that? What kind of black mahn is that who betrays his own mama?

5. [Y]ou mustn't waste your emotions on individuals, they don't count.

Answers: (1) [The vet, as he reminds the narrator to learn to "play the game" according to his own rules.] (2) [Dr. Bledsoe, telling the narrator that he is a fool if he thinks he can change the way things are. Bledsoe believes the narrator is better off learning to adapt to reality.] (3) [The high school superintendent, as he emcees the battle royal, telling the narrator that he must always remember his "place" as a black man in white society.] (4) [Ras the Exhorter, during his first encounter with the narrator and Brother Tod Clifton, urging the two to support their black community.] (5) [Brother Jack, revealing to the narrator his philosophy that groups, not individuals, are ultimately important.]

Essay Questions

1. What does *invisibility* mean in the context of this novel? Give examples of how the author depicts this invisibility within the story.

2. Beginning with slave narratives, the "running man" is a key theme in black folklore and literature. How does Ellison incorporate this theme into *Invisible Man*? (Consider: Why is the narrator running? What starts him running? What keeps him running? What is he running from? What is he running toward?)

3. Analyze the novel's three-part structure. How does it represent the narrator's movement from "purpose to passion to perception"?

4. Analyze Ellison's use of humor, satire, or irony.

5. Throughout the novel, Ellison plays on our tendency to define ourselves (and others) in terms of external elements such as physical characteristics and material possessions. For example, Brother Jack's glass eye symbolizes his limited vision; the narrator's calfskin briefcase symbolizes his emotional and psychological baggage. With this in mind, briefly describe the relationships between the following characters and the items or elements associated with them:

   a. Brother Tarp's leg chain and portrait of Frederick Douglass

   b. Mary Rambo's cast-iron bank

   c. Lucius Brockway's false teeth

   d. Reverend Barbee's white handkerchief

   e. The narrator's new suit

Practice Projects

1. Draw a map of Harlem that highlights the streets, clubs, neighborhoods, and other landmarks the narrator describes.

2. Write a follow-up to the novel that takes place six months after the narrator emerges from his underground hideout and rejoins society.

3. Create a Web site for *Invisible Man* that provides information and links on such things as the author's background, the setting of the novel, characters, symbols, and themes.

4. Write a letter from the narrator to his mother and father about one of his adventures in Harlem, convincing them that he is doing just fine.

5. Write an essay that examines the appeal of Communism and Black Nationalism for blacks living in a segregated society.

6. Listen to the song "Invisible" by the late Curtis Mayfield, included in his musical anthology, *People Get Ready: The Curtis Mayfield Story.* Then write an essay exploring how the song lyrics reflect the theme of *Invisible Man.*

CliffsNotes Resource Center

The learning doesn't need to stop here. CliffsNotes Resource Center shows you the best of the best—links to the best information in print and online about the author and/or related works. And don't think that this is all we've prepared for you; we've put all kinds of pertinent information at www.cliffsnotes.com. Look for all the terrific resources at your favorite bookstore or local library and on the Internet. When you're online, make your first stop www.cliffsnotes.com where you'll find more incredibly useful information about *Invisible Man*.

Books

This CliffsNotes book provides a meaningful interpretation of *Invisible Man* published by IDG Books Worldwide, Inc. If you are looking for information about the author and/or related works, check out these other publications:

Conversations with Ralph Ellison, edited by Maryemma Graham and Amritjit Singh, contains interviews with Ellison from 1952 to 1994. Supplemented by a comprehensive Introduction and a detailed chronology of Ellison's life. Jackson, Miss.: University Press of Mississippi, 1995.

Visible Ellison: A Study of Ralph Ellison's Fiction, by Edith Schor, provides insightful critiques of all of Ellison's fiction, from his early short stories to *Invisible Man*. Westport, Conn.: Greenwood Press, 1993.

Cultural Contexts for Ralph Ellison's Invisible Man, edited by Eric J. Sundquist, provides background information on some of the historical characters, events, and documents referenced in *Invisible Man*. It also offers insight into black folklore and culture, a comprehensive section on the history of Harlem, and an extensive bibliography of Ellison's writings. Boston: Bedford Books of St. Martin's Press, 1995.

African American Writers contains an essay titled "Ralph Ellison" by Robert G. O'Malley that provides a detailed look into Ellison's life and works. New York: Collier Books, 1993 (1991).

Blues, Ideology, and Afro-American Literature includes an essay by Houston Baker titled "To Move without Moving: Creativity and Commerce in Ralph Ellison's Trueblood Episode" that offers an innovative approach to the character of Jim Trueblood. Chicago: University of Chicago Press, 1984.

The Sermon and the African American Literary Imagination includes an essay titled "The Sermon without Limits and the Limits of the Sermon: Invisible Man" by Dolan Hubbard that analyzes Ellison's use of sermonic language and explores the role of the sermon in black culture. Columbia, Mo.: University of Missouri Press, 1994.

It's easy to find books published by IDG Books Worldwide, Inc. You'll find them in your favorite bookstores (on the Internet and at a store near you). We also have three Web sites that you can use to read about all the books we publish:

■   www.cliffsnotes.com

■   www.dummies.com

■   www.idgbooks.com

Internet

Check out these Web resources for more information about Ralph Ellison and *Invisible Man*:

The Literature and Culture of the American 1950s, http:// www.english.upenn.edu/~afilreis/50s/home.html— includes extensive links to information on Ellison and *Invisible Man*, including reviews of the novel from national media shortly after the book was published.

Random House Teacher's Guide, http://www.randomhouse. com/acmart/invman.html—lists several sample essay questions, discussion topics, and suggestions for related reading to help readers focus their analysis of the novel.

Decoding Ralph Ellison, http://www.igc.org/dissent/ archive/summer97/early.html—an online version of an insightful and comprehensive essay on Ellison by critic Gerald Early. His discussion includes *Invisible Man* and other works by and about Ellison.

Journal Resource

See this resource for more information about Ralph Ellison:

Hunter, Jeffrey W., et. al., eds. "Ralph Ellison." *Contemporary Literary Criticism* (Vol. 114), 1999: 84-139. Supplemented by an extensive bibliography, the essays in this volume provide a wide range of perspectives on Ellison's fiction and nonfiction.

Send Us Your Favorite Tips

In your quest for knowledge, have you ever experienced that sublime moment when you figure out a trick that saves time or trouble? Perhaps you realized you were taking ten steps to accomplish something that could have taken two. Or you found a little-known workaround that achieved great results. If you've discovered a useful tip that helped you understand *Invisible Man* and you'd like to share it, the CliffsNotes staff would love to hear from you. Go to our Web site at www.cliffsnotes.com and click the Talk to Us button. If we select your tip, we may publish it as part of CliffsNotes Daily, our exciting, free e-mail newsletter. To find out more or to subscribe to a newsletter, go to www.cliffsnotes.com on the Web.

Index

12 Million Black Voices, 10, 54

A

African American literature
  Br'er Rabbit tales, 24
  call and response, 9
  oral tradition, 10
  running man, 12, 29
  symbolism, 98
  trickery, 96
African American Writers, 113
Alice in Wonderland, 81
allegory, 10
allusions
  Alice in Wonderland, 81
  Black Boy, 45
  Huckleberry Finn, 31
  Julius Caesar, 69–70
  "Love Song of J. Alfred Prufrock, The," 32
  Moby Dick, 24
  Native Son, 93
  Odyssey, 73, 91, 96
  Popeye, 53
  Rene Descartes, 53
  riding race, 82
  wordplay, 24, 104
American Dilemma, An, 8
American Dream, 10, 28, 82, 98
animal symbolism, 61, 101
Antony, Marc, 69, 70
archetypes, 98
Armstrong, Louis, 22–23, 99, 109

B

Baker, Houston, 113
Baldwin, James, 5
bank, cast-iron, 56–57, 95, 98
Barbee, Rev. Homer A.
  described, 15, 39–40, 91–92
  imagery, mind/body separation, 41
  tokenism, 69
bartender. *See* Barrelhouse; Big Halley
battle royal
  described, 11, 26
  Golden Day chaos mirrors, 35–36

narrator's initiation in world of violence
    and brutality, 50
  riot similarities, 81
  struggle theme, 27–28
betrayal, 26
Bible, 100–101
bildungsroman, 8
Black Boy, 45
black community
  Harlem. *See* Harlem
  heat wordplay, 78
  homogeneous image shattered, 57
  movements, contrasted, 62
  responsibility, narrator's sense, 54
  selling out, 61
black vernacular, 53
blacks
  appearance and power, 62
  circus metaphor, 24
  color symbolism, 99
  commentary, 5–6
  criticism of novel, 8–9
  dolls, puppets and tokens, seen as, 67
  leadership profiles, 104–107
  literature. *See* African American literature
  manipulating, 61
  reality, dual, 10, 50
  sexuality and manhood, 30–31
  struggle for out-of-reach prize, 27
  veterans represent, 36
  wordplay, 102–104
Bledsoe, Dr. A. Hebert
  confrontation, 49
  described, 15, 90–91
  insult, 88
  power, 35, 41
  prejudice, 40
  quotation, 110
  tokenism, 69
  transformation, 34–35, 39
blindfolds, 28
blindness
  Brother Jack, 73, 96
  Rev. Barbee, 39, 41, 91–92
*Blues, Ideology, and Afro-American
    Literature,* 113
books
  author's other, 3–4
  black commentary, other, 5
  literary allusions. *See* allusions
  literary influences, 4–5
  resources, 113–114
boxing match. *See* battle royal

briefcase, 11, 26, 28, 77, 98
Broadnax, Mr. and Mrs., 15, 31
Brockway, Lucius, 17, 49
Brotherhood
    described, 8
    disillusionment, 13, 71–73
    falling out, 64–65
    independence, 70
    induction, 55–58
    joining, 13, 54
    Ras speaks against, 74
    rising role, 60
Bunch, William, 45
Burnside, 16

C

Caesar, Julius, 69–70
call and response, 9
car symbolism, 35
castration nightmare, 13, 110
Cervantes' *Don Quixote*, 3
chain links, 65, 98
characters, listed, 14–18. *See also individual
    characters listed by name*
Charlene, 16
Chthonian, 55, 57–58, 60
circus metaphor, 24, 26, 101
Civil Rights acts, 9, 50
Clifton, Brother Tod
    attack on white man, 64–65
    attacked by Ras the Exhorter/
        Destroyer, 60
    death, 13
    described, 17, 95–96
    doll-selling, 67–68
    funeral, 69–70
    identity, reminder of, 62
    relationship with narrator, 62
color symbolism, 23, 29, 98–100
Crenshaw, 16
Cyclops, 73, 96

D

Dante, 10
Decoding Ralph Ellison, 114
Divine Comedy, 10
dolls
    Clifton sells, 67–68
    people as, 27, 67
Dostoyevski's *Notes from Underground*, 3
double entendres, 104

Douglass, Frederick, 9, 63, 66, 82
dreams
    American Dream, 28
    castration nightmare, 13, 110
    Harlem, 45
    running man, 12, 29
Drew, Charles Richard, 50
Du Bois, W.E.B., 40, 62, 105
Dupre, 18, 80, 82

E

Early, Gerald, 114
Edna, 16, 37
education, 27, 40–41
Eliot, T.S., 4, 9, 32
Ellison, Ralph Waldo
    blacks in America, commentary, 5–6
    career highlights, 3–4
    Collected Essays of Ralph Ellison, The, 4
    Conversations with Ralph Ellison, 113
    *Cultural Contexts for Ralph Ellison's
        Invisible Man*, 113
    literary influences, 4–5
    personal background, 2
    racism in America, book review, 8
    Visible Ellison: *A Study of Ralph Ellison's
        Fiction*, 113
Emerson, Ralph Waldo, 4, 5, 34, 93–94
Emerson, Young Mr., 16, 44, 46
Emma, 18, 55
eulogy, 69–70

F

factory, 12, 44, 48, 81
fate, 23
feminists
    black, criticism of novel, 9
    suffrage movement, 66
fiction, blending with fact
    Booker T. Washington stories, 40
    overall, 24
    veterans tell stories, 36
    women's rights movement, 66
fight, staged. *See* battle royal
Fire Next Time, The, 5
Flying Home and Other Stories, 4
food, 43, 52–53
Founder, the, 15
Fourth of July celebrations, 82

G

Garnett, Brother, 18
Garvey, Marcus, 16, 94
gatekeepers, 17, 41, 49
Gates, Henry Louis Jr., 5
gender, 9, 66
gods, 100
Going to the Territory, 4
Golden Day
    color symbolism, 98
    microcosm of American society, 36
    mirrors battle royal, 35–36
    narrator and Mr. Norton visit, 12, 34
    narrator recalls, 84
    riot similarities, 81
Graham, Maryemma, 113
grandfather, 12, 14, 26, 89
Great Migration, 9, 107

H

Halley, Big, 16
Hambro, Brother, 17
Harlem
    Brotherhood abandons, 74
    narrator's initial view, 12, 43–46, 54, 109
    Renaissance, 107–108
    riot, 9, 13, 80, 82–83
heat wordplay, 78
Henry, Patrick, 69
Hester, 16
history, 24, 50, 70, 85
Homer, 10, 73, 91
hospital
    experiments, 12, 48, 109
    fear, 50
Hubbard, Dolan, 114
Hubert's wife, 18
Huckleberry Finn, 31
Hughes, Langston, 2, 9, 23
humor, 24, 81, 103
Hunter, Jeffrey W, 115
hyperbole, 103

I

identity
    food symbolism, 52
    narrator struggles, 8, 9, 57, 85
illumination, 23

imagery
    bank, cast-iron, 98
    birth, 50
    dolls and puppets, 27, 67
    Harlem riot, 81
    identity change, 57
    mechanical man, 32, 37
    mind, body separation, 41
    slavery, 65
insults
    chitterling eater, 88
    mother, 101
Internet. *See* Web sites, addresses listed
invisible man. *See* narrator
Invisible Man, The (H.G. Wells), 10
irony, 24, 28, 61, 103

J

Jack, Brother
    criticizes narrator, 56, 71
    described, 17, 96
    meets narrator, 53–54
    quotation, 110
    vision, losing, 73
Jackson, 14
Jemima, Aunt, 94
Juneteenth, 4

K

Kate, 15, 32
Kimbro, Mr., 16

L

leadership
    nature, 104
    Tarp demonstrates faith in narrator's
        ability, 63
    types, 104–107
light, 23
*Literature and Culture of the American
    1950s,* 114
Locke, Alain, 23, 107
"Love Song of J. Alfred Prufrock, The," 32
lynchings, 36

M

MacAfee, Brother, 18
MacDuffy, Mr., 16

Maceo, Brother, 18
machine symbolism, 32, 37, 101
manipulation tactics, 62
Matty Lou, 15, 30, 32
McConnell, Fanny, 2
Melville, Herman, 24
memories, 98
Men's House, 51
mob mentality, 81
Moby Dick, 24
moral absolutes, 30, 32
music
    author's studies, 2
    cart man, 43
    color symbolism, 99
    jazz structure, 29
    language, 104
    narrator imagines himself as accordian,
        51
    narrator's love, 22, 109
    reality, transcending, 23
    silence, 58
    Trueblood's, 92, 93
Myrdal, Gunnar, 8
myths
    American Dream, 28
    Cyclops, 73
    number symbolism, 100
    Santa Claus, 31
    sexually insatiable black man, 31, 37
    Sibyl, 78

N

NAACP. *See* National Association for the
    Advancement of Colored People
    (NAACP)
*Narrative of the Life of Frederick Douglass, an
    American Slave,* 9
narrator
    betrayal, 26
    black community, responsibility, 54
    Brotherhood career, 55–58, 60, 70–77
    Brotherhood, falls out, 64–65
    college expulsion, 34, 39
    described, 14, 88, 89
    emotional maturity, growing, 63, 68,
        73, 85
    eviction scene, 52–53
    Golden Day, visits, 34
    grandfather predicts future, 26

Harlem riot, 80, 82, 83
Harlem, arriving, 43–46
horror at hospitalization, 50
light, focus on, 23
Trueblood, visits, 30–31
underground home, 22
veteran of race war, 84
narrator's speech, 28
National Association for the Advancement of
    Colored People (NAACP), 62
National Book Award, 8
Native Son, 4–5, 9, 93
New York. *See* Harlem
New York University, 2
Nigger Jim, 31
Nobody Knows My Name, 5
North
    adjustment, 45
    characters, 16, 17, 18
    color symbolism, 100
    machine symbolism, 101
Norton, Mr.
    described, 14, 89, 90
    directions, seeking, 85
    Golden Day, visits, 34
    Trueblood, visits, 12, 30–31
Notes of a Native Son, 5
numbers symbolism, 100–101

O

O'Malley, Robert G., 113
Odyssey, The, 10, 15, 73, 91, 96
opportunists, 65
oral tradition, 10
oxymorons, 104

P

paint factory. *See* factory
party, 58
playing the dozens, 101–104
plot synopsis, 11–13
power symbolism
    battle royal, 28
    car, 35
    lesson, 40
    Trueblood understands, 93
    veterans, controlling, 37
primitivism, 107
prisoners, 36

pronunciation, 102
propaganda, racist, 28
protest novel, 4
Provo, Sister and Brother, 17
puns, 102
puppets symbolism, 27, 67

Q

quest narrative, 10

R

race
    movements, 62, 75
    power struggle, 28
racism
    covert, 14, 46, 89
    Ellison's book review, 8
    propaganda, 28
Rambo, Mary, 12, 17, 48, 55, 94–95
Random House Teacher's Guide, 114
Ras the Exhorter/Destroyer
    attacks narrator, 13, 74
    described, 16, 93, 94
    identity, reminds characters, 62
    initial contact, 12
    quotation, 110
reality
    Booker T. Washington stories, 40
    color symbolism, 99
    dreams symbolize retreat, 98
    escaping, 92
    inverted, 10, 103
    myths transformed, 31
    number 3 symbolism, 100
    transcending with music, 23
    veterans' stories, 36
    women's rights movement, 66
red color symbolism, 99
Red Summer, 36
regional differences. *See* North; South
religion
    fall back, 45
    reality, escaping, 92
    sermonic language, 41
Renaissance, Harlem, 107
repetition, 103
riding race metaphor, 82
Rinehart, B.P., 13, 18, 74–75
riot, 80, 81, 82, 83
running man, 12

S

Sambo, 67, 68, 94
Santa Claus, 31, 98
Schomburg Center for African American
    Culture, 108
school superintendent, 14, 110
Schor, Edith, 113
Scofield, 18, 80
segregation, 11, 50
self-image, 58, 65
selling out, 74
*Sermon and the African American Literary
    Imagination, The,* 114
sermonic language, 9, 41
Shadow and Act, 4
Sibyl, 78
Singh, Amritjit, 113
slavery
    allusions, 104
    chain links, symbolism, 98
    education, 40, 41
    Fourth of July celebration, 82
    ghost, 9
    imagery, 58, 65
    roles, 31
    running man theme, 29
    white man's burden, 89–90
socialism, 62
South
    characters, 14, 15, 16
    color symbolism, 100
    food, 44, 52–53
    machine symbolism, 101
spelling
    blonde, 104
    brief case, 104
Statue of Liberty, 49
Sundquist, Eric J., 113
Supercargo
    beating, 34
    described, 16
    power, 35
    symbolism, 37
Sybil, 13, 18, 77
Sylvester, 16
symbols/symbolism
    allegory, 10
    animal, 101
    battle royal, 28
    cars, 35
    chain links, 65

symbols/symbolism *(continued)*
color, 23, 98–100
dolls, 27, 67
Frederick Douglass, 9
Liberty Paints, 49
machine, 101
numbers, 100–101
overview, 98
sight, 73
synopsis, plot, 11–13

T

Tarp, Brother
described, 17
imprisonment, 64–65
leadership, faith in narrator's, 63, 109
Tatlock, 14, 37
Thomas, Bigger, 93
time
circular nature, 24
number 3 symbolism, 100
Tobitt, Brother, 17, 72
tokens, 11, 28, 67, 69
transcendentalism, 4–5
Trueblood, Jim
described, 15, 92, 93
narrator and Mr. Norton visit, 12,
30–31, 68
sacrifices self to protect family, 31–32
Tuskegee Institute, 2, 40
Tuskegee Study, 50
Twain, Mark, 31

U

understatement, 103
United Negro Improvement Association
(UNIA), 94

V

vernacular, black, 102–104
vet, The, 15, 43, 110
veterans. *See* Golden Day

W

Washington, Booker T.
character in novel, 15
compromises, 63
conflicting views, 40, 91
philosophy, 27–28, 40, 89
Waste Land, The, 4, 9
Web sites, addresses listed
CliffsNotes, vi
IDG Books, 114
resources, 114
Wells, H.G., 10
Wheatstraw, Peter, 45
whites
blacks, view of, 24, 67
Brotherhood members, 64
burder, carrying, 37
civilizing blacks, 89, 90
dual reality, 10
narrator thought were superior, 8, 88
reality, dual, 50
tactics used to manipulate blacks, 62
Trueblood understands power
structure, 93
Woman Question, 66
women, role of, 9, 54, 66, 94–95
wordplay
black vernacular, 102–104
English language, nuances, 24
heat, 78
names, 75
party, joining, 58
power, 45
Wrestrum, Brother, 18, 64
Wright, Richard
Chicago, initial view, 45
critical assessment, 5
Ellison, relationship with, 2, 4, 9
Harlem Renaissance, 107
Native Son allusion, 93
12 Million Black Voices, 10, 54
writer, 85, 107